ISLANDS ON THE ROCKS

*IMPETUS OF CHINA'S ACTIONS
IN THE EAST CHINA SEA*

RAHUL KARAN REDDY

Edited by
Asma Masood

Chennai Centre for China Studies

KW Publishers Pvt Ltd
New Delhi

Copyright © 2018
Chennai Centre for China Studies (CCCS)

The Chennai Centre for China Studies (C3S), registered under the Tamil Nadu Societies Registration Act 1975 (83/2008 dated 4th April 2008), is a non-profit public policy think tank with the following objectives.

- Carry out in-depth studies of developments relating to China with priority to issues of interest to India such as
  1. Geopolitical, economic and strategic dynamics of India-China relations.
  2. China's internal dynamics.
  3. The Sino-Indian border issue.
  4. China's relations with South Asian countries.
  5. Prospects of Sino-Indian economic and trade relations.
  6. Future evolution of China's politics and its impact on India and the world.
  7. China - India - ASEAN relations.
  8. China's emerging role in SAARC.
  9. Growing importance of South India for Chinese interaction and economic investment.
  10. India - China - Southeast Asia cultural links.
- Suggest viable solutions/policy alternatives on the basis of studies to the strategic planners and decision makers in India, on issues of bilateral, regional and global importance.
- Create public opinion, particularly in South India, on the implications arising out of China's emergence as a leading global power.
- Provide a forum for dialogue with China scholars in India and abroad and give space for expression of alternate opinions on China-related topics.
- Provide a sound data base for research on China with special attention to tapping information available in Chinese language material, so as to benefit scholars, media and think tanks in India as well as rest of the world.
- Address the requirements of the business community in India, particularly informing them about the nature of emerging business opportunities and problems while dealing with China.
- Liaise with think tanks specialising on China, both in India and abroad, with the objective of exchanging views.
- Organise lecture discussions and seminars on topics of current interest.
- Interact with institutions of higher learning in South India to create awareness about developments in China.
- Bring out publications relating to China - books, edited volumes, monographs and occasional papers.

ISBN 978-93-87324-03-9   Paperback
ISBN 978-93-87324-04-6   ebook

Published in India by Kalpana Shukla

KW Publishers Pvt Ltd
4676/21, First Floor, Ansari Road, Daryaganj, New Delhi 110002
Phone: +91.11.23263498/43528107
Email: kw@kwpub.com • www.kwpub.com

Printed and bound by Bhavish Graphics

Contents

Acknowledgements	v
Preface	vii
About the Editor	ix
Foreword	xi
Introduction	xiii
Overview of the Issue	xv
1. China's Trade and Commercial Links	1
2. China's Energy Concerns	7
3. Military and Research Activity in the ECS	12
4. Sino-Nationalism over the ECS	22
5. Japan's Position on the ECS	29
6. Conclusion	44
Notes	53

List of Maps

Fig 1: Disputed Territory in the East China Sea	xiv
Fig 2: PLAN Fleets and HQ	13
Fig 3: The First and Second Island Chains	38

Acknowledgements

Producing this monograph required the support and input of friends, co-workers and family members whose contributions have been vital. I would like to thank Asma Masood for guiding me every step of the way and giving me the freedom to choose the structure and focus of my paper. I also wish to express my appreciation and thanks to Commodore Vasan and Sundeep Kumar for their inputs and suggestions which were practical and constructive. I would also like to thank Mr. L.V. Krishnan for his help in gathering data and for directing my study. I am grateful to the Chennai Centre for China Studies for allowing me to work on this project and giving me the opportunity to work as an intern. I would like to thank Ram Karan for his inputs and support which have been critical to the completion of this paper.

Preface

Maritime disputes are fast becoming a source of tension and conflict in Asia. This trend is a symptom of the global economy and international order rebalancing itself toward Asia. The rise of China, India and other Asian economies has generated economic gains that have a correlation with increased military presence and power projection. This is most observable in the case of China, which is the principle claimant in the East China Sea (ECS) and South China Sea (SCS). With China acting aggressively to dictate the rules of engagement, other Asian economies are not far behind in terms of responding in the same way. Japan and China are on a collision course in the East China Sea and regional maritime security is at risk of being destabilised for the sake of power projection.

The maritime commons have become increasingly valuable for the flow of trade and energy supplies. China's stake in the ECS is subject to strategic insecurities and vulnerabilities like the Malacca Strait dilemma and the island chain containment, which have prompted the Chinese state to act to eliminate these vulnerabilities and insecurities. Applying its strategy in the ECS, the Chinese state has altered the regional security of Northeast Asia and impelled Japan into remilitarising itself.

About the Editor

Asma Masood is a Research Officer with the Chennai Centre for China Studies (C3S). She holds an M.A in International Studies from Stella Maris College, Chennai and a B.A in Journalism from M.O.P Vaishnav College, Chennai. Her areas of research span China's foreign policy, India-Myanmar-China relations and soft power.

Foreword

There is enormous focus on the happenings in the South China Sea (SCS) due to the aggressive posturing of China and its cartographic aggression, combined with it carving out of artificial islands from the rocks and reefs. The increased attention to the happenings in the SCS is obviously due to the greater number of players with stakes in the maritime areas of the SCS. However, in the case of the East China Sea (ECS), the two major players are China and Japan and, by and large, the issue is bilateral as opposed to the multilateral issue in the SCS.

From that point of view, this study by Rahul Karan Reddy brings out the related issues and complexities of the dispute between China and Japan in the ECS and the impact on regional security and stability. The headings under which Rahul has covered the complexities include economic relations, energy security, military posturing and strategic impact. I must complement Rahul for bringing out the related issues with an academic rigour that was demanded while dealing with the subject. Rahul's stint in the Chennai Centre of China Studies during his internship has equipped him to deal with the topic with confidence. This work will also help Rahul in his future endeavours as a researcher and hold him in good stead.

The study of China's behaviour, whether in the SCS or in the ECS, helps in understanding the manner in which China deals with its maritime neighbours to buttress unsubstantiated and illegal historical claims. It is essential for both nations to work towards conflict resolution by enhanced Confidence Building Measures (CBMs) and cooperation. From that point of view, the recommendations made by the author are of great value in addressing the core concerns of the two nations without allowing these to impact peace, tranquillity, economic engagement and development.

This monograph, doubtlessly, would be an invaluable reference document for students, academia and researchers. I also would like to take this opportunity to wish Rahul all success in his future academic endeavours.

Commodore **R. S. Vasan** IN (Retd.)
Director, Chennai Centre for China Studies (C3S)

Introduction

China's actions in the East China Sea (ECS) comprise a strategy to project control of the Senkaku/Diaoyu Islands. Beijing's actions in the region hint at economic insecurities as well. To ensure that these insecurities do not manifest in harm towards Chinese interests, the Chinese military apparatus, notably the People's Liberation Army – Navy(PLAN), has displayed firm and absolute control over the region. Japan has regularly alleged that the PLAN vessels, Coast Guard ships, fishing boats and research vessels demonstrate their ability to assert control and act aggressively here. Notably, Japan has not recognised the Chinese claim to sovereignty and maintains that the islands do not comprise disputed territory. Tensions in Sino-Japanese relations over the hydrocarbon resources and effective control of the islands have periodically intensified and given the international community cause for concern.

Fig 1: Disputed Territory in the East China Sea[1]

Courtesy: Wikimedia Commons

Overview of the Issue

I. China's commercial activity in the East China Sea (ECS) is a vital economic pillar for the country. Its manufacturing sector, concentrated along the eastern coastal region, is the factory for the export and import of billions of dollars of goods[2]. The export oriented model of China's economy necessitates unhindered access to sea lanes for the transmission of trade. The East China Sea and its sea lanes comprise one of the windows to the global economy for China's production and consumption.

II. China's oil and Liquefied Natural Gas (LNG) are imported through sea lanes that eventually reach the East China Sea after passing through the Strait of Malacca and South China Sea. Maritime choke points in the South China Sea are vulnerable to blockades and are currently embroiled in disputes and tensions. The stability of energy supplies in the ECS is one of the first steps in eliminating China's energy insecurity. In addition, the discovery of hydrocarbon resources in the region has raised the stakes and increased China's assertiveness over energy supplies in the ECS. To survey the resources in the ECS, China's maritime agencies have dispatched vessels to obtain oceanographic data[3], conduct echo testing[4] and carry out seabed surveys[5] in the territorial waters of Japan. China displays an interest in the resources available for exploitation and is intent on carrying out resource exploitation in the face of protests lodged by the Japanese government[6.] Beijing's energy policy reveals a hunger for resources and a dedication to locate and secure alternative energy routes and supplies which project potential threats.

III. The East China Sea is one of China's immediate theatres of operation, and establishing control here is vital to the country's image as a global power, to the international community and its domestic polity. Cumulatively, these various considerations have directed China's actions and behaviour in the ECS.

This occasional paper seeks to answer the following research questions

- Why is the East China Sea of economic interest to China?
- How does the ECS figure in Beijing's energy security calculus?
- What military and scientific measures is Beijing taking to ensure control of the ECS?
- What national interests does China seek to protect?

1
China's Trade and Commercial Links

First, a broad overview of China's economic strength is crucial to understand the insecurities that it harbours. China's economy has grown rapidly over the last decade and growth currently stands at 6.9 percent[7]. A closer look at industrial clusters on the East China Sea coast will reveal the basis of Chinese economic growth. It will also throw light on why it is crucial for China to maintain stability in the ECS. The country's economic growth, to an extent, can be attributed to three industrial clusters on the eastern and southern coasts of China. The Yangtze River Delta, Pearl River Delta and Bohai Rim are strategic zones that house industrial parks of three kinds: Economic and Technological Developmental Parks (ETDPs), Hi-Tech Development Parks (HTDPs) and Eco-Industrial Parks (EIPs).The Yangtze River Delta alone contributes to 18.5 percent of China's Gross Domestic Product (GDP) (2014)[8]. The three industrial parks in 2009 were responsible for 54.5 percent of the GDP[9] and they have been scaled up since. For the purposes of this paper, the Yangtze River Delta and Bohai Rim will be the focus of study because they are situated on China's eastern coast and look out into the ECS.

The Yangtze River Delta straddles three provinces: Zhejiang, Shanghai and Jiangsu, covering less than 2.2 percent of China's land, contribute 35.5 percent to Chinese exports and imports (2016)[10]. In 2011, the Yellow River Delta alone handled 83.7 million tonnes of foreign trade cargo and 54.5 million Twenty-foot Equivalent Units (TEUs) which account for 34 percent of China's exports and 37.6 percent of China's export volume[11]. The main mode of facilitating exports in the Yellow River Delta is through maritime trade routes in the East China Sea. Ports along the east coast are, therefore, vital for the transmission of Chinese exports[12]. Any instability in the ECS will affect the outflow/exports from these industrial clusters, thereby undermining China's economy. Therefore, a close study of these industrial clusters and their economic value is necessary.

The two provinces of Zhejiang and Jiangsu have extensive transportation networks connecting them to 12 ports in the Shanghai International Shipping Hub (SISH)[14]. The ports service the fast-growing industries of the Yangtze River Delta that export goods from the ECS coast. Shanghai and Ningbo are the busiest of these ports. Cargo is either directly sent to Shanghai and Ningbo or is trans-shipped there through smaller feeder ports like Nanjing, Nantong, Zhapu and Zhangjiagang[15]. Chinese ports are responsible for 30 percent of the world's total trade throughput and world exports[16], the largest and fastest growing of which are along the ECS.

Shanghai is the most important intersection for trade in Asia. It is an international hub in Northeast Asia and the prime source of imports from Japan, Hong Kong, the USA, Netherlands and Korea[17]. The city is the national distribution centre for imported consumption commodities, accounting for 30 percent of China's imported consumption commodities. Beyond Northeast Asia, China's eastern ports also play a key role in the export of goods to destinations like the United States, the European Union (EU), Hong Kong and India, which received the bulk of Chinese exports as of February 2017[18].

Looking at these facts and figures, it is evident that the Chinese foreign trade system has come to depend on shipping as its main method of transporting and receiving goods. In fact, it must be noted that of the world's ten biggest ports, seven are located in China[19], of which four are located along the east coast.

Sea lanes and shipping are important in this context because shipping is the most efficient mode of transport. High-value products like industrial machinery and equipment for light goods like clothing and footwear are cheaper to transport through sea-borne vessels. Both product types constitute the bulk of exports from China to the USA, Japan, South Korea and Taiwan[20]. Maritime transport costs are less for short distances as well, making maritime trade between China and Japan, Taiwan, South Korea and other East Asian nations relatively cheaper.

In this context, China exports automatic data processing machines, electric apparatuses, parts and accessories for motor vehicles, TV receivers, LCDs, optical appliances and instruments: these are the most common goods China exports via the ECS[21].

It may be China's intention to control the maritime trade routes in the East China Sea so that it may shape the balance of power in East Asia. The East China Sea will carry more global trade in the next two decades and its sea lanes will become more populated as well, appreciating in strategic value.

Bilateral trade relations between China and its East Asian neighbours are predicted to increase and further diversify by 2030, making the ECS increasingly valuable for the flow of regional trade[22]. In fact, China's bilateral trade with the USA, Japan, Korea, India, Singapore, Hong Kong, Indonesia, Malaysia, Nigeria and Thailand figures in the 30 largest bilateral trade pairs[23]. This trend could work in Beijing's favour, increasing other nations' economic dependence on China and accentuating China's influence on their behaviour.

Beijing will be in a position to take advantage of East Asia's reliance on it as a market and supplier. There is a possibility of Beijing withdrawing investments from, and trade cooperation with, any nation that objects to its 'peaceful' rise. The ECS lanes are one of the means to keep trade flowing between China and its partners. The ECS issue that has flared up in the last two decades and received international attention, may continue to feature in the security agenda of East Asia for the foreseeable future. This is problematic for China because the safety of its exports and imports is not guaranteed as long as the ECS poses a security risk.

Maritime traffic in the ECS will increasingly carry the imports and exports of China, making Chinese economic growth increasingly dependent on sea trade. This may prove to be a vulnerability for China in case Japan decides to build a military base on the Senkaku Islands. The future of maritime trade for China looks promising but Beijing's concerns over security in the Sea Lanes of Communication (SLOCs) in the ECS will only increase, making its behaviour more assertive and aggressive.

Threatened by the possibility of a blockade or military intervention by any of its neighbouring states, China seeks to preemptively eliminate any threat to its economic supremacy. Even a minor change in sea routes to subvert a blockade will raise the prices of its exports in the international market, making products less competitive. In view of the current tactic of 'cartographic aggression' that China has adopted to safeguard its economic advantages and opportunities, it is safe to say that China will seek to dominate the ECS so as to maintain leverage in the regional economy.

One aspect of this economy is the fishing industry, with China being the largest exporter of fish products in the world. Fish is central to the dietary needs and livelihoods of the coastal fishing communities. The industry boasts of 695,000 vessels and is the largest producer of wild catch and seafood, making fish the largest agricultural export from China[24]. The industry keeps expanding because the Chinese government provides subsidies to the tune of USD 4 billion for its fishing fleets[25]. The largest of all the fisheries is located in Zhejiang, adjacent to the ECS. Here, the port of Shenjiamen is the national centre for deep sea fishing[26] and a docking site for boats that fish in other international waters.

Interestingly, Chinese fishing fleets are encouraged to ply outward to help strengthen Beijing's territorial claims in the ECS. The Chinese government turns a blind eye to fishing fleets that enter the waters of the Senkaku Islands in search of fish. Doing so, propagates a claim for Chinese sovereignty. The push outward is also driven by the immediate realities of maritime resources' production dwindling after years of overfishing near China's coastline[27]. Fishing is essential for the people of rural China along the coast, and their advance into the territorial waters of the Senkaku Islands is supported by the state. Large fishing fleets, fuelled by nationalist sentiments and under the protection of the Chinese Coast Guard, represent another form of Chinese economic expansion in the face of threats to the fishing industry.

There are other vulnerabilities regarding the ECS affecting China's economic performance and interests. Namely, fuel for economic growth. Energy security has been a core component of Chinese national interests since the 1980s. The full extent of its energy needs was realised after China opened its markets to the world in 1978. It drastically raised China's domestic and industrial requirements for oil and gas. The need to discover, secure and exploit energy sources has been a driving force behind China's actions in the ECS.

2
China's Energy Concerns

China's dramatic increase in industrial production and consumption has strained its national energy resources. The energy demands of its industrial bases have rendered its energy reserves insufficient and economically unfeasible to exploit. To keep industries producing, China has had to import energy from the Middle East, North America, South Asia and Africa. Over 20 years, from being a net exporter of oil and gas, China has become a net importer of all these resources. China imports 50 percent of its oil from the Middle East[28]. It also imports one-third of its gas supply[29].

To escape the risks of complete dependence on foreign sources of energy, China has been on the lookout for new energy reserves to reach a balance between self-sufficiency and energy diversity. The ECS offers China an opportunity to achieve this goal by exploiting the hydrocarbon resources underwater. Ever since the discovery of hydrocarbon resources in the ECS in 1969, the race to claim territory in the ECS has accelerated and taken new forms[30].

China's behaviour in the context of the ECS dispute indicates a quest for energy self-sufficiency within its immediate sphere of influence. The problem of energy supply has bothered Chinese policy-makers, military officials and strategic planners because of the 'Malacca dilemma'. China has stimulated a policy of diversifying energy sources and routes while also looking for sources of energy directly under its control. However, China's energy concerns arise closer to the mainland.

This is evident as the East China Sea is estimated to contain 200 million barrels of oil in proven and probable reserves. On the other hand, China claims that the undiscovered resources can be as high as 70-160 billion barrels of oil[31]. The ECS basin has significant natural gas deposits, estimated at 1 and 2 trillion cubic feet (tcf)[32]. China's ventures reveal gas reserves of 119 billion cubic feet (bcf), a promising find that is currently being developed as a joint venture between the China National Offshore Oil Corporation (CNOOC) and a UK firm[33]. The Pinghu field's output currently stands at 40 million cubic feet (mcf) per day[34]. The prospect of energy resources in its own backyard has motivated China to act decisively and exploit them. China has gained a foothold in the region by being the first mover to exploit the oil and gas reserves. This has set a precedent for further incursions into the contested waters.

In the contested waters close to the median line proposed by Japan, China has expanded its exploitation of hydrocarbon resources by building rigs near the Okinawa trough. Close to the Okinawa trough is the Chunxiao/Shirabaka field, the largest gas field in the ECS. It constitutes twelve oil platforms that China has installed[35]. Most of these platforms have been operationalised in recent years, undermining security in the region for the sake of energy. By gradually expanding operations into the contested waters, China has made its intentions to exploit resources in disputed waters clear and overt. The expansionist tactic works to create a precedent for incontestable exploitation. It also improves the historical basis for China to claim that it has always exploited resources in the ECS as a part of its own territory.

In addition, the ECS would help China's most important industrial bases and highest energy consuming areas – Zhejiang, Shanghai, Jiangsu, Anhui, Hebei and other provinces on the east coast that have no energy resources of their own. They have had to rely on imports from the northern and western provinces, which is relatively costly and largely insufficient. The ECS provides a feasible alternative to land-based pipelines and ports that China has been building across Central and Southeast Asia. A steady supply of energy to industrial bases on China's east coast, through the ports of Shanghai and Ningbo,[36] is sustaining the industrial growth.

The geopolitics of natural gas in the ECS has worked in China's favour. The Chinese side of the median line has favourable operating conditions because of greater depth (44m average depth). China has, therefore, been able to conduct the bulk of resource development in the ECS. Oil and gas from the ECS can be transported to China's coastal provinces faster and more economically than to Japan[37]. The cluster of rigs is 5 km from the median line that Japan uses to delimit the maritime boundary between China and Japan[38]. Hence, China can continue to exploit these resources without having to compete, and share them, with competitors in East Asia.

The unilateral development of resources in the contested waters allows China to further its claim of sovereignty over the Diaoyu Islands. The lack of a concrete framework to deal with joint development and maritime boundaries in the ECS creates space for China to establish its presence. Increased presence in the region will amplify the illusion of control, strengthening China's claim of sovereignty over the ECS and emboldening it with every subsequent provocation and infringement. Strategic aggression in the form of oil rigs equipped with radars and protected by air and sea power solidifies China's control over the vital resources[39]. It also deters other claimants from carrying out resource exploitation in the same waters. These factors will encourage China to normalise its expansion into ECS waters by using oil rigs, potential naval bases and other infrastructure in the future.

Apart from allowing China to cultivate a claim for sovereignty through hydrocarbon resource exploitation, the ECS is also a gateway to access long-term sources of energy that have not yet been exploited or explored. The Arctic is one such destination.

Simply put, China can open up new maritime routes that subvert the problem of maritime chokepoints in East Asia, by controlling the ECS. The Northern Sea route is an opportunity for China to circumvent the problem of blockades[40]. It also opens up new trade routes with Europe for its energy supplies. According to the *Polar Journal*, "Maritime trade from East and North China can reduce travel time to European ports like Rotterdam by re-routing their ships through the Northern Sea route. Travel time from ports like Nanjing to Rotterdam through the Northern Sea is shortened by six and a half days. Estimates by scholars at the Shanghai Maritime University put savings at USD 60-120 billion if China makes use of Northern Sea shipping routes"[41]. Clearly, control over the SLOCs in the ECS is critical for the future of Arctic shipping from China's perspective.

However, any Arctic exploration and exploitation for oil and gas has been deemed by Chinese officials as impossible to carry out without dealing with Russia[42]. Russia's stance on the ECS dispute is unclear. Like China, Russia too regularly enters the waters of the Senkaku Islands, which indicates the possibility of Russia also not recognising Japan's sovereignty over these islands. However, Russia has made no claims to the ECS. In fact, Sino-Russian military cooperation occurs in the region, as will be discussed in the following chapter.

Joint research and development of oil and gas resources around Russia and gradual inroads into shipping in the Northern Sea will bear fruit only when China secures its SLOCs in the ECS first. It is only then that the Arctic will prove to be a feasible destination for China's energy trade. A cooperative and cosy relationship between China and Russia is imperative for such a long-term objective. The stakes are high when it comes to Arctic shipping and, hence, it is clear that Arctic shipping will be possible only through a security consensus with Moscow regarding the ECS. These stakes are evident as China has made inroads into the Arctic shipping and energy market by investing in drilling companies owned by countries with a foothold in Arctic shipping[43], including Russia.

To develop a security consensus and an axis of convenience, China and Russia have sought to demonstrate collective security and cooperation in the realm of energy security. Other engagements with Russia have implications for the ECS as well, specifically in the military and research dimensions.

3
Military and Research Activity in the ECS

Resource engagements with Russia constitute a significant component of Sino-Russian relations, but other elements of the relationship also shape the power balance in East Asia. Joint military exercises have been cited as an important aspect of the China-Russia relationship. The military dimensions emphasise considered cooperation between both nations in the face of Western interventionism. An instance of the solidarity can be observed in the joint island-seizing exercise conducted by the Russian Navy and the PLAN in the South China Sea in 2016, one day after the Permanent Court of Arbitration (PCA) ruling invalidated China's territorial claims in the South China Sea[44]. The timing of the exercise cannot be ignored. It serves to display preparedness in case of conflict escalation, and demonstrate the military strength and operational readiness of the PLAN. China is capable of conducting similar exercises in the ECS as well, in case Japan takes the case of the Senkaku Islands to the Permanent Court of Arbitration.

Russia also supplies arms to China and provides technology that has helped modernise the PLAN. Russia has sold approximately USD 750 million worth of arms to

China[45]. The PLAN has modernised its weapon systems and phased out older obsolete vessels. Modernisation and advancement of technological prowess have paved the way for a new naval doctrine, especially applicable to the ECS context.

Fig 2: PLAN Fleets and HQ[46]

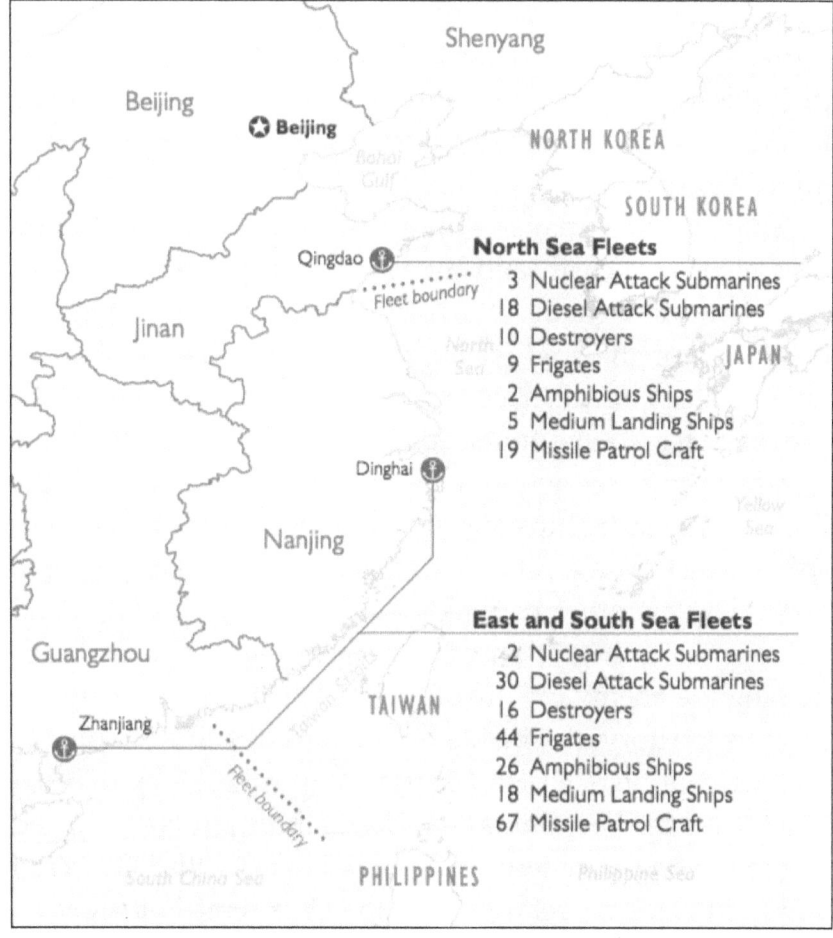

Courtesy: U. (n.d.). China- Military - Major Naval Units [Map]. In Perry Castaneda Map Collection. Annual Report to Congress. Retrieved from http://www.lib.utexas.edu/maps/middle_east_and_asia/china_major_naval_units-2012.png

The traditional strategy of the PLAN was "offshore waters defence", which was not restricted to the ECS, but always described in geostrategic terms by Chinese military officials and policy-makers[47]. This strategy has undergone a revision. China now describes its strategy as "open seas protection" with no geographic limitations on its scope. The PLAN's posture is active defence and applicable along its periphery to all landmasses and waters that Beijing claims as Chinese territory. Active defence as a posture includes striking first in case an attack is expected. It looks to effectively control situations in the ECS and firmly guard China's sovereignty.

Unlike older naval strategies, open seas protection necessitates a clear and unobstructed passage through the first island chain, which includes the ECS waters. To break out of the first island chain, Beijing has embarked on a strategy of deterrence in the ECS[48], which means the use of force to neutralise the operating capacity of the adversary's forces without direct combat. In the ECS, the PLAN's superior ships and submarines prevent Japan from countering Chinese actions. It calls for a display of power in ways that lets other nations know of China's strength and willingness to adopt an offensive strategy. It also means making the enemy unsure of the nature of China's action in its own territory. An incident that captures this position is the interception of a US aircraft on May 19, 2017, by two SU-30 jets over the East China Sea. The Chinese pilots conducted unprofessional manoeuvres, flew 145 m from the US aircraft and performed barrel rolls over the US aircraft[49]. It shows a willingness to engage in risky and confrontational behaviour, if only to project strength or to confuse adversaries and keep them guessing.

China prefers to use its civilian maritime law-enforcement agencies to protect its claims in the ECS. The agency responsible for this is the Chinese Coast Guard[50]. The mainland coast of China is more than 300 nautical miles (nm) away, but the use of the Coast Guard instead of the Navy indicates a strategy to push its putative defence perimeter outward. The anti-access strategy has been thickened in the ECS by beefing up the capabilities of the Chinese Coast Guard which is often the agency that infringes on the territorial waters of the Senkakus. It attempts to legitimise the Senkakus and ECS waters as Chinese coastal territory. This anti-access strategy is based on the principle of deterrence. The use of deterrence instead of war-fighting as the mode of operation requires the application of the space, cyber and naval assets at China's disposal. This has been prescribed in Chinese official documents brought out by the People's Republic of China (PRC).

The 2015 Defence White Paper outlines a strategy of winning local wars under highly informationised conditions[51]. Beijing's military capabilities reflect the same logic. An evaluation of China's counter-space assets indicates its progressive and modern nature, which aims to achieve deterrence[52]. The Dong-Ning 2 is a ground-based, high earth-orbit attack missile that was launched in 2013[53]. It wipes out enemy satellites orbiting the earth. It disrupts the navigational ability of the enemy's forces, rendering them incapable of operating. A closer look at China's counter-space programme shows the use of several technologies that can aid Beijing's deterrence policy in the ECS. Examples of its Anti-Satellite (ASAT) programmes include kinetic and directed energy like lasers, high powered microwave and particle beam weapons[54].

To improve its navigation and mapping capabilities, China employs multiple satellite navigational and tracking systems like the Global Positioning System (GPS), Global Navigation Satellite System (GLONASS) and China's own BeiDou-1. The BeiDou-2/Compass system is a far more advanced system with global coverage and is expected to be operational by 2020[55]. China is also planning eight satellites in the Huanjing programme that are capable of infrared, multispectral and synthetic aperture radar imaging. These space assets can identify and track ships and similar targets on the ground, and are effective in deploying naval assets in strategic areas[56].

Significantly, this array of space technology can be employed to track the movements and operations of Japanese vessels in the ECS waters. Knowledge of Japan's patrols and patterns of deployment gives China a tactical advantage. It allows its naval assets to be deployed in contested regions of the ECS to deter Japanese and US vessels from operating, thereby eroding the effective control of Japan.

Deterrence is also achieved using information technology and cyber warfare. The prongs of the strategy ensure lack of actual combat and contact between forces in the ECS. PRC military writings highlight the seizure of electromagnetic dominance in highly informationised conditions to ensure battlefield success[57]. The central component of informationised warfare is the use of Integrated Network Electronic Warfare (INEW), which gives China the ability to seize control of situations simply by knocking out the information systems of the adversary[58].

The anti-access strategy is, therefore, in accordance with the 'peaceful rise' of China, simply because it compromises the offensive capacities of adversaries without the use of force[59]. In addition, the latest function of China's anti-access strategy is its cyber warfare capabilities.

China's cyber warfare capacity has gained strength since 2010 and it has established an online presence by having the largest number of users on the internet[60]. In the domain of cyber warfare for military purposes, China has made significant advances too. Cyber warfare is rooted in the application of Net-Centric Warfare (NCW), Electronic Warfare (EW) and Computer Network Operations (CNO)[61]. Anti-satellite weaponry, jamming, over-the-horizon targeting and radar are available to China as part of NCW[62]. Other tactics include hacking into military networks to delay the deployment of forces, which constitutes the CNO branch of cyber warfare. The above capabilities are most commonly used to steal information from industries strategically significant to military strength, and intellectual property, like trade secrets as is the case with Japan and the USA. In recent years, China has also established information warfare units to develop viruses, trojan horses, worms and malware like GhostNet, Titan Rain and Operation Aurora to attack enemy computer systems and networks[63].

Several manifestations of these capabilities have been observed. After the nationalisation of the Senkaku Islands by Japan, 19 Japanese government websites were attacked by Chinese hackers[64]. This served as retaliation for the actions of Japan. Since the attack came from civilian hacker groups, the Chinese government could claim deniability. The integration of civilian and military units yields benefits for China and cautions Japan from undertaking any action in the ECS. Similarly, a US-based cyber security firm reported that a cyber attack targeted US officials who visited the USS *Ronald Reagan* in 2016. The attack came one day before the PCA ruling on China's South China Sea claims[65]. It is possible that China will attempt the same strategy in the ECS, if Japan begins the process of settling the dispute through international legal mechanisms. The attacks work to showcase an emboldened Chinese effort to target military assets. Such attacks are growing in number and targeting sensitive information. The attacks typically make no effort to conceal their intentions.

Japan has reason for profound concern, as two large Signals Intelligence (SIGNIT) facilities in Shanghai operated by the PLAN are capable of intercepting signals and communications in the ECS. These facilities could be used to launch a cyber attack, disrupting Japan's Command, Control, Communications, Computers, Intelligence, Surveillance, Reconnaissance (C4ISR) capabilities. Such cyber attacks in the ECS would be highly effective in demoralising the Japanese Navy. In fact, Japan reported 24.5 billion cyber attacks in 2014, 40 percent of which reportedly came from China[66]. Another series of attacks comprised mostly data breaches in the defence industry and hacking of Japanese Diet members' email accounts[67]. The units acting in the interest of China are elements of the civilian militia and PLA network operators, creating linkages in the structure of China's cyber warfare capacity[68].

The attacks sow confusion, irritate adversaries, damage networks and databases, and often steal valuable data. China reportedly used phishing attacks on Mitsubishi and 20 other defence and hi-tech companies in Japan to steal classified information[69]. The attack took place on Manchuria Day (September 18), a day of national humiliation at the hands of the Japanese. This cyber attack was likely in revenge for the historical atrocities committed by Japan. Tokyo has sought to combat such attacks through selective multilateral cyber security frameworks and reorienting its cyber security posture to be more offensive[70]. Any act by Japan to assert its control over the Senkaku Islands is, hence, likely to provoke China into launching a cyber attack. US intervention in the ECS will evoke a similar response.

Applied together, the prongs of the anti-access strategy also achieve Beijing's long-term goals of extending its command and communication capacity beyond its coasts. It gives the PLAN logistical and communication support to carry out operations in the Pacific, beyond the second island chain. The ECS is valuable from a strategic standpoint for China because it will serve as a command and communications centre for its blue water Navy.

China's cyber, space and communication technologies also enable military and scientific research in the ECS. The data and information gathered is put to use to give China better operational advantage in the ECS waters. But in the name of research, China has managed to extend its naval ambitions and claims of sovereignty.

Research and Scientific Exploration
As per an agreement signed in 2001 between China and Japan, the two countries are to each notify other about vessels conducting scientific research near the coastal waters of the respective state[71]. However, despite this agreement, to notify the other state about carrying out research in the ECS, scientific research and Intelligence, Surveillance, Reconnaissance (ISR) activity has been undertaken by Beijing without notifying Japan[72]. This often evokes strong responses when submarines are noticed trailing Japanese naval vessels

and US aircraft carriers[73]. Chinese vessels have been spotted conducting research for days at a stretch, without any notification to the Japanese government[74]. Besides, Beijing has not revealed the nature of the research being conducted in the ECS. If the SCS is to serve as a precedent, China could be planning an underwater base or research station to assert its claims in the ECS[75]. If the proposed underwater base in the SCS is to serve as a blueprint, a base in the ECS can be expected to be operational for months at a time.

The technology of China's research programmes is ambitious and quite sophisticated. It gives Beijing advantages in the ECS that bolster its claim to sovereignty and strategy of deterrence. Research vessels give the State Owned Enterprises (SOEs), that carry out drilling, data about the quantity of resources and information relevant to exploit the maximum amount of resources in the shortest time[76]. It also facilitates the ISR apparatus of the PLAN. The importance of carrying out research can be observed by the number of incursions made in the ECS by Chinese research vessels, which has more than doubled in 2015, from 9 to 22, as reported by the Japanese Foreign Ministry[77]. Other instances involving submarines and Unmanned Aerial Vehicles (UAVs) have been reported, gathering data about the ocean floor, echo-sounding and seabed surveying[78].

Like China, the other littoral states such as South Korea have established research stations on rocks that are submerged at high tide in the ECS. The station is used for weather pattern detection, to aid navigation of ships, and provide early inputs on natural disasters[79]. Japan conducts research in the waters of the ECS as well, often eliciting reactions from Taiwan and the littoral states surrounding the ECS. Hence, research in the ECS is common, but the nature of the Chinese scientific research is unprecedented and far more aggressive.

It should be noted that a cabled seafloor unmanned observatory is already operational in the ECS. Live data is being streamed from this observatory[80]. The average depth of the ECS is much less than that of the SCS[81], making an underwater lab much more viable. It needs to be emphasised that the proposed lab in the SCS will be an unprecedented operation that will demonstrate China's technological and scientific superiority in Asia. It could also signal the establishment of a base in the ECS.

Similarly, the use of underwater drones implies research and technological capability that can be utilised in the ECS for the benefit of China's control. The drones are deployed with the help of submersible craft, the most capable of which have been built by China[82]. These craft can be used to deploy Upward Falling Payload (UFP) programmes that place drones on the ocean floor. They are non-lethal, deep sea nodes that are remotely activated when needed and enable a full range of maritime mission sets that are more cost-effective than existing manned or long range unmanned naval assets[83]. China's plans to become a technological superpower by 2030 are being realised through deep sea research and technology. The possibility of deploying payload systems, underwater bases and submersible manned vessels in the ECS is high and will improve Beijing's presence in the region.

The above factors have highlighted the tangible strategic dimensions of China's ECS actions. However, there are also ephemeral yet significant domestic factors which motivate China's actions in the ECS, as will be elucidated in the next chapter.

4
Sino-Nationalism over the ECS

Nationalism in China has intrinsically been tied to its history. China's recent path to rejuvenation has given nationalism the momentum to assert itself in the context of Asia-Pacific geopolitics. Chinese nationalism now bears a distinctive mark of pride, bolstered by two decades of economic growth. Any upset in China's global position or a retraction of China's position in the ECS would prove detrimental to the reputation of the CCP (Chinese Communist Party). Backing down in the ECS to Japan or the USA would come across as a loss of face to the Chinese people, something they are not likely to tolerate amidst the atmosphere of glory and a revitalised national spirit, with the aim of restoration of the former grandeur.

Deep-seated mistrust and animosity that mar Sino-Japanese relations have been revived in the Senkaku Islands dispute[84]. Chinese animosity towards Tokyo has been largely triggered by Japan's actions concerning the Senkaku Islands. Japan's nationalisation of the islands in 2012 sparked violent protests in major cities across China[85]. Protests took place outside the Japanese Embassy in Beijing, the likes of which turn violent when Japan acts in ways that are perceived as a return to its imperialist and militaristic past.

The protests involve vandalising Japanese businesses and destroying goods made in Japan. Chinese protestors often call for a boycott of Japanese goods. However, a boycott cannot be sustained for long due to the economic interdependence between the two nations, and the lack of substitutes would hurt the Chinese economy as well. While this makes the boycott counter-productive, it nevertheless, sends a political message. For instance, after the anti-Japan protests in 2012, Japanese car makers decided to temporarily shut down the factories[86]. This was a significant move because China's automobile industry is the largest market for Japan's auto industry. The protests have hampered trade to a fair degree—not enough to cause serious damage to the economy of either country, but enough to limit the operation of Japanese businesses on Chinese soil to a fair degree.

Another economic repercussion was seen when Japan, the biggest importer of China's rare earths, was affected by the sudden fall in the global exports of rare earth minerals from China in 2010[87]. However, it is not clear if the fall in exports was instigated by the Senkaku Islands dispute or was a planned move unrelated to the tensions with Japan. All the same, it caused significant panic in Japan when the prices of the minerals quadrupled. A great degree of economic interdependence is at risk of regressing if nationalism gets in the way of economic interests. The issue of sovereignty in the ECS legitimises violent Chinese nationalism, at the cost of economic cooperation and trade relations. Hence, the CCP is careful in stirring anti-Japan sentiments among the Chinese people.

The anti-Japan nationalism is also an instrument of foreign policy to highlight social preferences in China so that the CCP is legitimised to act in ways that achieve the national and social preferences.

Anti- Japan grievances are inculcated among the Chinese from their formative years. The state-run patriotic education campaign of the Chinese government is mandatory from kindergarten through college and it supplements museums, monuments and historical sites. It is the method of inscribing the memory of the Sino-Japanese War (1937-45) into the national psyche[88]. China works to keep the memory fresh in the popular culture in order to achieve its larger goals in the ECS. The programme has generated a brand of nationalism in China based on the injustices suffered by the Chinese. It inculcates an attitude of hostility, reinforced in the face of disputes in the ECS. Nationalism is a carefully calibrated force in China, where the CCP's attitude towards a protest depends on the nature of the issue and its target. Protests on certain domestic issues such as ethnic identity are not tolerated, while anti-Japan protests are allowed to take place[89]. The CCP, hence, legitimises certain protests based on its necessity to achieve national interests. The above stated tendency of the protest culture allows anti-Japan nationalism to operate with confidence in China. Nationalism is encouraged by another element of the CCP's agenda: the rejuvenation of Chinese glory.

The Chinese Dream is an idea of restoring China to its former glory and has been the centrepiece of China's ambitions. Restoration of Chinese territory lost in the Sino-Japanese War(1894-95) is a fundamental objective of the Chinese Dream of national rejuvenation. Sovereignty is held as a key Chinese national interest and Beijing has made it clear that it will not budge on its territorial claims[90]. The Senkaku Islands dispute is, above all else, a dispute over territorial sovereignty and, therefore, ignites the strongest nationalist sentiments. The sentiments are given substance when Japan is perceived as hindering China from revitalising its glory, namely, when Tokyo reiterates its control over the Senkaku Islands.

The historical consciousness behind Chinese nationalism is subverted to legitimise the actions of China in the ECS and to decry Japan's actions. Moreover, it gives China deniability. Nationalism works as a bargaining chip to claim that China is doing what is necessary to maintain internal stability. Additionally, nationalism has found new ways of expression, beyond the CCP's control: the advent of cyber groups that advocate strong nationalist sentiments and promote Chinese nationalism on the internet, and that have threatened to operate outside the purview of the CCP's preferred limit[91].

The umbrella of Chinese nationalism encompasses diverse discontented groups that could challenge and attack the current leadership in the case of economic mismanagement, corruption or, above all, if the CCP softens its stance on Japan. The Chinese people would not stand for a lenient stance on Japan, especially one that deals with China's claims to territory in the ECS.

To appease its nationalist elements, China often undertakes policies and passes laws that may reflect an aggressive and uncompromising stance to the rest of the world. This has become the policy practice since the late 1990s. Interestingly, it was not so during the normalisation of Sino-Japanese relations in 1978. China claims that an agreement was reached during the talks between Deng Xiaoping and Takeo Fukuda (Prime Minister of Japan, 1976-78), that the two sides would shelve the territorial dispute and pursue joint development[92]. This could be interpreted as a compromise by Chinese leaders for better Sino-Japanese relations.

At that time, it was in China's interests to cooperate with Japan to make the 'Open Door' policy a success. Technological knowhow from Japan was essential for the success of the Chinese economy. Maintaining friendly relations and checking nationalist tendencies were in the interest of China's rejuvenation. Under such cirumstances, and pressure from the USA, the previous generation of Chinese politicians decided to shield diplomatic relations from instability by eliminating the source of conflict: nationalism over the Senkaku Islands.

In contrast, in 1992, when the military apparatus of the CCP needed to assert its claims over the Senkaku Islands it passed a domestic law: the Law on Territorial Seas and Contiguous Zones. The law explicitly states that the Diaoyu Islands lie in Chinese territorial waters. It must be noted here that a key determining factor is the control of nationalist elements (the military) on internal politics and how they shape the foreign policy of China toward the ECS. An acceptable foreign policy depends on domestic support for national interests, which the military is more likely to represent[93]. Nationalism in China can influence issues of foreign policy.

This scenario was evident when a tug of war took place between the PRC's Ministry of Foreign Affairs and the Chinese military over whether to explicitly include the Diaoyu Islands in the law. The military's explicit suggestion was to include the islands[94]. However, the Ministry of Foreign Affairs did not want to compromise on the visit of the Japanese Emperor to China which was to take place shortly after the law was to be passed. The importance of the 20th anniversary of the normalisation of the Sino-Japanese relations was overridden by the military. The Chinese military was able to get its way because its recommendation was in line with the nationalist atmosphere in which hardline, fundamental and nationalistic assertions were more likely to gain public support.

It is likely that the final decision was made by Jiang Zemin[95], who was looking to consolidate his vulnerable support base by supporting the hardline nationalist military position. In all likelihood, it made sense to make a nationalistic choice, to gain support from the military and from the public. Zemin's actions are confirmed by his widespread implementation of patriotic education and his clear hardline stance on Japan in the following years[96].

Sino-nationalism is mobilised to achieve foreign policy goals, at the cost of bilateral relationships between China and other states. Violent nationalism makes China's relationships with its regional trading partners tense and unstable. It is also detrimental to Beijing's dream of rejuvenation because the respect that China expects from the rest of the world will not be given if China strains relationships using its domestic politics. This is detrimental to the national interests of the Chinese state. A conciliatory and negotiating stance is lacking in the foreign policy doctrine, which is why China fails to make progress with its neighbours regarding territorial disputes. Soft power diplomacy has a better chance of eroding the alliance system of its neighbours with the USA and help Beijing in achieving its national interests.

Fuelling deep historical wounds and taking a hardline stance on disputes stakes the CCP's reputation on an outcome that is still unsure. Beijing is raising the expectations of its polity by promising not to back down from the Diaoyu issue which compels the CCP to achieve no outcome short of complete sovereignty. An outcome that doesn't satisfy the anti-Japanese nationalist sentiment will turn out to be problematic for the CCP when the people realise they have lost out to the Japanese yet again. The CCP would face the threat of increased criticism. It would make matters worse if the Chinese economy enters a recession. Corruption in the CCP has already drawn flak from the people, and economic mismanagement in the form of foreign investments going bust will affect the CCP's control over the nationalism. The pre-conditions are present for Sino-nationalism to spiral out of control and, if it does so, it will dent the legitimacy of the CCP. This would strengthen Japan's position in the ECS.

5
Japan's Position on the ECS

Japan has enjoyed effective control over the Senkaku Islands since the Okinawa Reversion Treaty of 1971[97]. In the face of recent Chinese incursions to invalidate its effective control over, and peaceful ownership of, the islands, Japan has maintained a calm and composed stance towards China in the ECS. Tokyo has simultaneously responded to Chinese remarks and actions in firm and equal measure, though it has not recognised the disputed status of the Senkaku Islands[98]. Tokyo is also prompt in dealing with Chinese fishermen and Coast Guard vessels that enter the territorial waters of the Senkaku Islands, and has scrambled jets to intercept Chinese aircraft flying over the islands and other Japanese territory[99]. Japan's military response has shown the country's willingness to stand up to Chinese aggression and secure its own territory. The Japanese government has demonstrated to the international community that in the light of historical facts and international law, the Senkaku Islands belong to Japan. Tokyo has also registered its protests with the Chinese government and continues to argue its case using the framework of international law.

The economies of China and Japan are well connected, and conflict in the ECS can be detrimental to the interests of both states. However, the ECS issue is unlikely to hamper economic interdependence between China and Japan. Both economies have a similar model and function on a rule-based international trade regime.[100] Even during the height of the Senkaku Islands crisis in 2012, Japanese exports to China comprised 17 percent of Japan's total trade. After 2012, the proportion of exports to China compared to total trade has increased (to 20-22 percent), demonstrating strong economic interdependence between the two states even during times of friction.[101] In the same year, trade relations between both states appeared to be full of opportunity.

Over the last few years, a flurry of economic interdependencies has been created. China's largest home appliance company, Haier, announced that it would set up its Asian headquarters in Japan.[102] Similarly, Mitsubishi Corporation announced that it would team up with a Chinese company to develop an iron ore mine and wharf in Australia.[103] Japanese car manufacturer, Mazda, announced that it would expand its Chinese dealership. Toyota also announced that it would relocate its Headquarters (HQ) from Japan to Beijing.[104] It is clear that economic interdependence and commerce will take precedence over politics and guide the future of Sino-Japanese cooperation. Trade and commercial linkages between Beijing and Tokyo are a pillar of stability for Sino-Japanese relations though other elements of Sino-Japanese relations may occasionally disrupt cooperation.

The stability of economic interdependence will be determined by the ECS issue to some extent, but Japan is fairly certain that Beijing will not tamper with the SLOCs security in the ECS. Doing so would cause a breakdown in

Sino-Japanese economic cooperation, which will not work in Beijing's favour. On account of Japan's geographical proximity, technological knowhow and capital, Japan is essential for the modernisation of the Chinese economy.[105] For Tokyo, a significant way to keep the Chinese economy relatively dependent on Japan is through technology transfers.

One such area of cooperation is the High-Speed-Rail (HSR) technology that Japan's train industry is known for. Kawasaki Heavy Industries (KHI), the maker of the Japanese bullet trains (*Shinkansen*) has signed a technology transfer agreement with CSR Sifang, the builder of China's high-speed rail programme.[106] The technology transfer from Japan to China has benefited China and enabled it to compete in the global market. China has been able to secure a USD 5 billion contract to build Indonesia's first high-speed rail and is currently competing with Japan to bid for the rail link between Singapore and Kuala Lumpur.[107] Technology transfers from Japan to China will restructure the Chinese economy in the near future and are the glue of economic interdependence between Japan and China. Tokyo can rest assured that its technology and production quality will keep the Chinese economy vested in Japan. However, Japan is bent on competing with China for economic influence in Asia.

Tokyo's economic strategy is about investing in the states party to the SCS dispute, which strengthens Japan's position in the ECS by consolidating efforts against Chinese aggression.[108] Japan has sought to counter China's economic influence in South Asia through its sponsored and co-financed projects executed by the Asian Development Bank and other regional multilateral fora. Investments made by Tokyo for geothermal energy, natural gas pipelines, technical assistance, transportation and urban development projects are being funnelled through the Asian Development Bank[109] in India (Kashmir and Northeast India), Myanmar, Philippines, Mongolia, Central Asia, Indonesia, Vietnam, Cambodia and Bangladesh. The projects compete with Beijing's strategy of investment to cultivate economic influence. Industrial competition in the areas of renewable energy, robotics and electric cars is being played out in Asia, specifically in countries party to the SCS dispute. By investing across Asia in competition with China, Japan has displayed its economic prowess as well as its ability to influence actors using economic strength.[110] Tokyo is confident of its ability to sway the support of the Southeast Asian states away from China towards Japan. The conscious decision to unite the ECS and SCS disputants against China has been taken by Japan in its economic strategy.

Tokyo even extended its reach as far as Africa, at the Sixth Tokyo International Conference on African Development, where Shinzo Abe pledged USD 30 billion in public and private support for African development. USD 10 billion was allocated for infrastructure projects executed in cooperation with the African Development Bank.[111] The strategy to integrate support for Japan's position in the ECS by providing investment and monetary support has caught Beijing's attention.[112] It prompted a response from the Chinese Ministry of Foreign Affairs which claimed that Japan was imposing its will on the African countries to drive a wedge between China and these countries. Japan has also attempted to insert the issue of maritime cooperation and security into the Yokohoma Declaration on Japan-Africa cooperation.[113] Tokyo's strategy of commitment to multiple regional and international fora rivals Beijing's attempts to do the same with the Asian nations and simultaneously causes a spillover of a territorial dispute to the economic realm.

Japan's direct investment in the Association of Southeast Asian Nations (ASEAN) countries is comfortably higher than inflows from China.[114] As Beijing and Tokyo vie for influence in ASEAN and other regional fora, Japan is bundling the ECS dispute with the SCS one to challenge the general tendency of Chinese aggression faced by nations involved in maritime disputes with China. Japan has sought to bring together all the parties opposing China in the SCS, through investments and Overseas Developmental Assistance (ODA). Shinzo Abe also announced that procedures for ODA loans will be reduced while simultaneously stressing the traditional competitive advantages that Japan holds over China – safety, technology and integrated benefits.[115] Japan is attempting to demonstrate a responsible and superior investment package. This apparently does not occur in China's case due to suspicions among recipient states regarding the intent of investments.

The question of energy security is persistent in the foreign policy of Japan. However, another of Tokyo's concerns related to energy security is Japan's imported energy sources and routes passing through the Malacca Strait and other chokepoints that threaten the energy trade. The problem of chokepoints affects Japan too and under such pressures, Tokyo has sought to improve its energy self-sufficiency. The issue of energy self-sufficiency has called for a more active foreign policy from Japan with respect to the East China Sea.[116]

The issue of energy insecurity gained prominence especially after the Fukushima Daiichi disaster of 2011.

Japan increased its imports of LNG after the disaster amidst a wave of anti-nuclear campaigns, putting pressures on existing sources of energy supply.[117] Crude oil provides for 49.5 percent of Japan's primary energy needs, followed by LNG (22.7 percent) and coal (27.7 percent), all of which are imported from the Middle East and Africa.[118] Two years after the disaster, the share of nuclear generated energy fell from 15 percent to less than 1 percent and had to be covered by LNG imports.[119] The import dependence of Japan's energy mix rose from 80 percent to 94 percent. Japan has sought to reduce its reliance on coal and LNG by developing renewable energy sources that would diversify its energy mix and also reduce its import dependence. Japan has acknowledged its dependence on other countries for its energy needs, prompting the government to set a target for self-development of resources to the tune of 40 percent.[120] A flood of investments over the last five years has aimed to secure this objective.

The projects are an exercise in diversifying Japan's energy mix and diverting energy supplies from choke points to secure routes. A considerable number of these diversification investments have to do with renewable energy, mostly solar and wind farms. Tokyo wants to implement this long-term strategy of diversifying existing sources of energy and maintaining the proportion of nuclear energy at 20-22 percent, by 2030.[121] Renewable energy has been the subject of investments and innovation in Japan, sought as a long-term alternative to traditional energy sources. The domestic market in Japan has welcomed foreign companies willing to set up power plants. Support from Japanese banks for power projects at the domestic level and abroad, has shown a willingness to transform Japan's energy mix.

For instance, a US energy company, GSSG Solar, will build a solar power plant in Suwa, Nagano Prefecture, with an output of 47 MW, the bulk of which will be financed by borrowings from Shinsei Bank.[122] The French oil giant Total is set to construct a solar power plant in Nanao, Ishikawa Prefecture, in 2017.[123] In addition to economic benefits for Japan, these international energy deals offer Tokyo geopolitical advantages. Namely, a balancing act toward China. To add to the diversification of energy sources, Japan has embarked on a project to increase the efficiency of energy production, distribution and consumption.

The need for resources is strong in Japan, as seen when a Tokyo based drilling company was given rights to drill in the ECS.[124] The decision to grant the company rights was a reaction to Chinese SOEs commencing the construction of oil rigs in the ECS. The ECS provides a solution to diversify energy resources. Tokyo has been firm about resource development in the ECS despite the Chinese government setting up oil and gas platforms close to the contested territory. Since the operating conditions in the ECS are not favourable for Japan to conduct oil and gas exploitation, the Chinese are currently dominating this sector. For Japan to extract some benefits from the ECS oil and gas fields, an agreement similar to the one signed in 2008 will have to be engineered with the Chinese. The 2008 Japan-China Agreement on Cooperation for the Development of East China Sea Resources was the framework for potential cooperation in energy development which can ease both China's and Japan's concerns about energy resources in the ECS.

Japan has invested in the pipelines that extend from the gas fields in the ECS to Shanghai and Ningbo—a way of investing in the oil deposits.[125] However, no attempt at Sino-Japanese joint development of hydrocarbon resources has yet achieved a breakthrough. China's hard stance in the ECS has left no room for compromise. It is, therefore, in Japan's interest to pursue cooperation regarding hydrocarbon resources. Measures like sharing of information will build confidence and can work in the favour of regional security, provided the Chinese government can agree to them.

Similar to China's attempts to set up pipelines and alternative routes for energy trade, Japan has embarked on a project to invest in geothermal plants and other diverse sources of energy. USD 188 million was spent through ASEAN on electricity, gas and steam supply projects.[126] Japan has also sought to invest in Africa and other oil rich states to build new linkages in energy supply for the diversification of energy. However, these moves do not mean that Japan's prospects of energy from the ECS are dim.

The availability of energy in the ECS gives Japan an opportunity to address its energy security and build a cooperative relationship with China on the basis of energy development. The lack of an agreeable solution to the ECS energy dispute is a thorn in the side for Japan's energy security, and finding an agreement with the Chinese will assuage Japan's energy security concerns.

Japan's response to repeated violations of sovereignty in the ECS by the Chinese has been proportional and consistent. China's attempts to drill holes in the ECS security structure operated by Japan has evoked strong objection and criticism from the Japanese. Tokyo's counter-militarisation of the ECS is postured directly to deal with

Chinese aggression and power projection. To respond to repeated violations of its territorial sovereignty, Japan has begun to fill security vacuums on its Western island chains and is keeping a close watch on the situation around the Senkaku Islands.

A radar station on Yonaguni Island was installed recently to gather intelligence on Chinese vessels operating in the vicinity of the Senkaku Islands.[127] The radar station will aggravate China, and Tokyo has sought to do exactly that. The government in Tokyo has expanded the scope of the operation and capacity of the Japan Maritime Self-Defence Force (JMSDF) stationed around the Senkaku Islands for a faster response to China. Tokyo has also militarised the Nansei Islands in an attempt to beef up its ISR capabilities. Plans to reinforce Japan's anti-missile systems by 2020 are underway as well, by including the THAAD (Thermal High-Altitude Area Defence) system in Japan's three-tier ballistic defence system which includes the SM-3 interceptors and PAC-3 Patriot rockets.[128] The Japanese Coast Guard will receive a special unit of 12 ships to monitor the ECS and counter new Chinese Coast Guard ships.[129] Other vessels of the JMSDF such as the Aegis ships will receive upgrades and will have the SM-3 missile system.[130]

Fig 3: The First and Second Island Chains

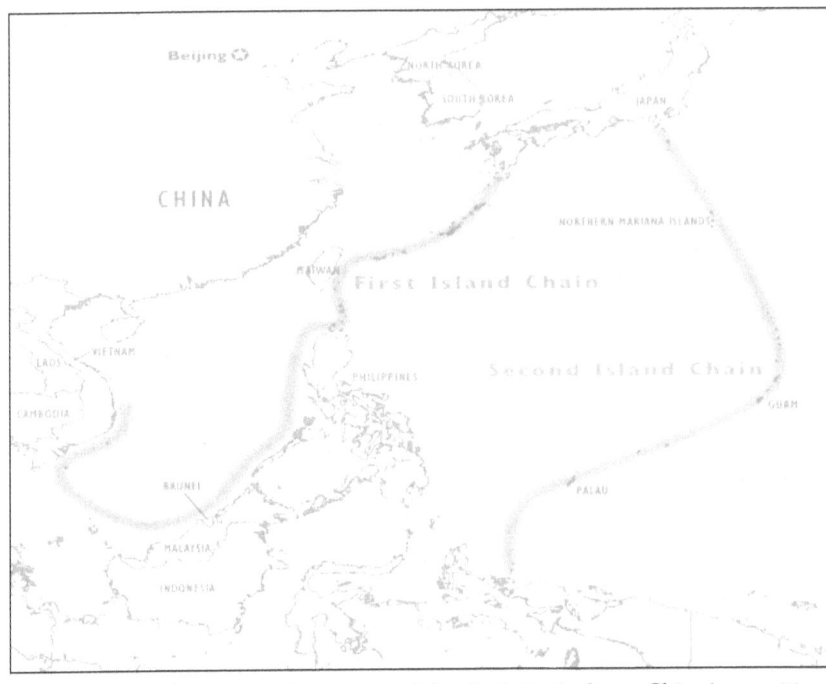

PRC military theorists refer to two 'island chains' along China's maritime parameters. The First Island Chain includes Taiwan and the Ryukyu Island the Second Island Chain extends from Japan to Guam.
[133]Island chains surrounding China, *Courtesy*: U. (n.d.). First and Second Island Chain [Map]. In Perry Castaneda Map Collection. Annual Report to Congress. Retrieved from http://www.lib.utexas.edu/maps/middle_east_and_asia/china_first_and_second_island_chains-2012.png

To contain China directly in the ECS, and counter its aggression, Japan has broadened its strategy by roping in nations that have maritime disputes with China. The disputants in the SCS also face Chinese maritime aggression against which Japan has sought to build a coalition of voices. Japan has decided to send its Izumo helicopter carrying warship to the South China Sea for three months of port visits before conducting drills in the Indian Ocean with the US Navy.[131] Tokyo has reached out to other South

Asian countries by lending them patrol vessels and training aircraft, and conducting joint exercises with their Navies.[132] By projecting power outside the ECS, Japan has indicated to Beijing its intentions to contain Chinese aggression in Asia.

The alliance between Japan and the USA has been mobilised as a power projection tool as well, deterring China from acting unilaterally to displace the status quo of the Senkaku Islands. In the event of an armed clash between China and Japan, Tokyo has prepared its islands as springboards to launch an attack on the Chinese mainland.[134] In the case of a preemptive strike from China, Japan can neutralise the missiles and other targets from the island defences. Militarising the furthest islands in the Japanese island chain has been an objective since the dispute escalated in 2012. The alliance with the US is a powerful strategic deterrent, which can halt Chinese attempts to change the status quo. Joint naval exercises and sharing of military information and capabilities gives Japan the advantage of mobilising the largest military power into action.[135]

Simultaneously, Shinzo Abe's government is also in a position to revise the constitutional limitations on the military of Japan. The government in Japan is keen on restoring the military's former size and glory, in the face of Chinese aggression. The revision would give the Japanese military the freedom to conduct operations and pursue strategic goals that would directly confront China and its ambitions.[136]

Japan has initiated a process to re-equip its military and the posture of its operation. The Self-Defence Force (SDF) was created to operate only as a defensive unit. However, security threats in the Asia-Pacific region have compelled changes in the military policy of Japan. The revised National Defence

Programme Guidelines point to a dynamic threat environment surrounding Japan and express the need to revise the operating capability of Japan's armed forces. The National Defence Programme Guidelines were revised in 2010 and again in 2013 to include collective self-defence and long-range ISR capacities to the SDF's operating capability.[137] The terminology and principles of the National Defence Programme Guidelines also reflect more dynamic and fully armed forces of Japan, envisioned to be characterised by readiness, mobility, flexibility, sustainability and versatility. The programme was revised to be a demonstration of national will and strong defence capabilities. The following years have seen defence expenditure growing to build new defences and expand the scope of existing ones. An amphibious unit has been in the works to strengthen Japan's capability to defend remote islands. F-15 fighter aircraft were moved to Okinawa to rebalance the outlook of Japan's external security. Military technology and goods have been purchased as well, including 42 F-35 A aircraft, P-1 long range patrol aircraft and a replacement for the Hyuga-class destroyer.[138]

The complete outlook and posture of the SDF is changing, under the pressure of Chinese aggression. Japan's military outlook and capacity has evolved significantly over the last decade and by 2020, the process is outlined to be complete. The development has placed China squarely in the middle of Japan's foreign policy and the government is motivated to engage with China. Japan will actively look to extend its operating capability to reflect its strength and willingness to counter Chinese aggression. The plan to revise the Constitution and reinstate Japan's military in its full capacity[139] will mean that significant political will has been mobilised against China. Though much work remains to be done for Japan's military to become a full-fledged force, a constitutional revision will also mean that the Japanese military will act out in stronger and more dynamic ways in the ECS.

Japanese nationalism, like nationalism in China, is being mobilised to achieve political ends. The coverage in Japan's leading newspapers regarding the island dispute has surged dramatically during times of tension. The language and content used to describe China and its actions have become stronger and taken a hardline stance.[140] A similar pattern has emerged in the opinions polls conducted in Japan during 2016 by the Pew Research Centre which measures that 86 percent of views are unfavourable towards China.[141] The ECS dispute has been a prominent and explosive issue for politics in Japan.

The nationalism generating the potential of territorial disputes was first utilised by the Liberal Democratic Party (LDP) as an election platform in 1996. Today, the LDP is seen as a revisionist political party that has stirred the ECS dispute with controversial moves like visiting the Yasukuni Shrine, nationalising the islands and encouraging right-wing nationalist groups. Though the media in Japan is not as tightly controlled and supervised as in China, the LDP government exerts a covert influence. The freedom of press rank held by Japan has been consistently falling which indicates a nationalist sentiment in the coverage of events related to the ECS.[142]

Japan's wave of nationalism has generated a movement to revise the Constitution and thereby change the status of Japan's sovereign right to use war as a means of persuasion. Article 9 – known as the peace clause of Japan's Constitution—does not allow the state to possess offensive military capabilities. The LDF government in power has sought to revise this by 2020 to embark on a project to remilitarise Japan.[143] Support for this move has not been strong, but the aggression from China is driving opinions to root for the revision of the Constitution. The move has a nationalist support base that calls for a stronger stance on China, among other things. More importantly, a stronger position on China in Japan's domestic politics has been voiced by neo-conservative members of the Diet Parliament.[144]

The parliamentarians perceive that Japanese youth lack patriotism and have emphasised the importance of the SDF, the constitutional amendment to normalise Japan's international status, and the populist policy of Shinzo Abe's government.[145] Japanese politicians prefer a moderate level of nationalism that would support their actions to counter Chinese aggression. However, a high level of nationalist rhetoric in the Japanese media does not work in the favour of the government because it may lead to international consequences and limit political options. Nationalism in Japan has gained momentum partly due to domestic politics, but also because Japan is asserting its authority and image in Asia-Pacific geopolitics, often directly opposing China, its historical adversary.

Japanese public action groups and students' federations have taken the Senkaku Islands dispute into their own hands by constructing a lighthouse on the islands. These groups express a strong nationalist policy and hardline stance in dealing with China. They have been the agents responsible for instigating the dispute which the government in Tokyo has channelled to its benefit and advantage.[146] Citizens and groups advocating stronger action against China have also increased in number, leading to the formation of nationalist groups. The right-wing groups in Japan that have been responsible for installing the lighthouse,[147] visiting the islands and attempting to purchase the islands have been the biggest beneficiaries from nationalism in Japan.

Japan's position in the ECS has been to display peaceful and effective control over the Senkaku Islands. The strategy has been to disable China from cultivating any claims to sovereignty so that Tokyo can exercise exclusive economic rights granted by international law. Japan's actions have been, on the whole, more notional and symbolic. They have psychologically antagonised China, resulting in greater aggression from China in the ECS. This action-reaction dynamic works in Japan's favour. It gives Tokyo the advantage of appearing like a peaceful and understanding neighbour, with a respectable track record of peaceful administration of the Senkaku Islands. Japan has acted with greater consideration for regional security and demonstrated the ability to hold its own against China's aggression.

6
Conclusion

The ECS is a vital strategic space for China and as a rising power, Beijing will seek to control the region. It is natural for China to flex its muscle in the ECS and project power. This behaviour is explained by a correlation between the increase in a nation's economic strength and increase in its military capabilities, as applicable in China's case. However, China's behaviour cannot be categorised based on the above factor. In fact, China's conduct in the ECS is an attempt to defend its economic, energy and nationalist insecurities and eliminate vulnerabilities. The outcome of maritime security and the Senkaku Islands dispute in the ECS will either make China susceptible or set it on a path of maritime aggression.

China is altering the balance of Asia to its advantage to become a regional economic and military heavyweight. Taking advantage of East Asia's economic dependence on China's exports and consumer market, Beijing is trying to draw countries in East Asia into its sphere of influence. For this to have an effect on the behaviour of other states, Beijing has sought to maintain a robust consumption market. It has also positioned itself as an indispensable link in the supply chain of goods and services.

The ECS fits into Beijing's calculations because of its SLOCs and the volume of trade in the ECS that pertains to East Asia's economies. Beijing would like to retain control and supervision of these trade routes as a source of leverage against the East Asian economies. More importantly, China would like to be certain that no other state, specifically US allies South Korea and Japan, establishes bases on the Senkaku Islands, thereby giving an advantage to the USA's early warning systems. It would also give the USA an opportunity to organise a blockade of trade in the ECS, adversely affecting China's economy.

In times of a blockade or crisis in the ECS, the sea lanes carrying oil and gas to China will become ineffective and limit its economic functioning. Eliminating energy insecurities by diversifying routes and securing existing ones immunises Beijing from blockades and foreign pressures on the energy market. Although Barack Obama's 'Pivot to Asia' has come to an end, the USA's presence in Asia as a response to North Korea or Chinese naval aggression makes China's energy supply lines vulnerable to disruptions. The main consideration for Beijing is to ensure that it is not boxed in, and its energy routes are not cut off completely, thus, placing Beijing in a weaker bargaining capacity.

To remain in control of its energy and routes of energy, Beijing has set in motion a strategy of maintaining military dominance in the ECS. It gives it control of energy exploitation in the ECS and energy supplies that come from the Middle East and Africa. The ECS is the first step to ensure unobstructed access to the energy markets in the Middle East. The SCS, adjacent to the ECS, is also witnessing such a strategy where the PLAN controls the waters to prevent any disruptions to energy supplies and trade routes. Beijing plans to solve this Malacca dilemma by breaking out of the containment imposed by the island chains. A Navy that can navigate out of the ECS, into the Indian Ocean and the Arctic will give China the freedom to secure new energy sources. A capable PLAN stands to ensure the safety of China's energy security.

The PLAN's actions in the ECS are precedents of a strategy to apply naval strength for the security of maritime trade and consistent energy supplies. The Navy has been a relatively subdued force in China until the recent past. Financial backing and improved technology have pushed the rise of China out into the ECS, with ambitions to command a blue water Navy. Equipped with a strong Navy and emboldened by its economic growth, China is not hesitating to defend its interests both at home and abroad. China's Navy has given it the confidence to challenge disputed territories openly, and undermine alliances. The ambitions of a blue water Navy indicate an urge to break out of the island chain containment and rebalance Asia in Beijing's favour. The PLAN's operations are going to demonstrate control in the ECS and beyond, in the near future. The ECS partly propels the beginning of Beijing's strategy to break out of its current limitations and acquire a Blue Water Navy.

Research in the ECS is another form of power projection simultaneously enabling China's capabilities in the region. Research bases and operations are supported as a part of the deterrence strategy. They supplement the infringements of the Chinese Coast Guard and root Chinese presence in disputed regions. Underwater bases in the SCS demonstrate Beijing's superior technological capabilities and an unfazed attitude toward claiming territory. Research operations present Beijing with an advantage over adversaries in the region, facilitating superior intelligence and better operational effectiveness.

Similarly, nationalism is a tool of Chinese foreign policy to secure support for its actions in international politics. Domestic support legitimises Beijing's actions but also puts at stake the reputation of the CCP on the outcome of events, such as the sovereignty of islands in the ECS. For Beijing to expect results, it has to look for cooperation and interaction between states with a consistent emphasis on soft power. There are prominent cultural linkages between Japan and China which Beijing can enhance at the state level. Antagonising the anti-Japan sentiments will backfire on the CCP in case the ECS dispute doesn't yield a satisfying outcome.

Anti-Japan nationalism has significant consequences for Sino-Japanese cooperation and economic interdependence that are at risk. By legitimising violent protests detrimental to cooperation and business linkages, China is harming its own economic credibility. It could also erode the image of a business-friendly environment in China, which may dissuade investors. Chinese nationalism is likely to erupt when disputes with other nations reignite, leading to instances of vandalism, looting and destruction of businesses of other states, as has been observed earlier. Nationalism of this kind cannot sustain itself if China wishes to be a prominent destination for investment and a market for foreign goods. Repeatedly aggravating the populace in China to project popular support for Beijing's actions will exhaust domestic support. If the outcome of disputes does not go in China's favour, the CCP will have to face a disgruntled polity that will seek to vent its frustration.

Despite the above vulnerabilities and insecurities that the ECS manifests for China, Beijing may be on the verge of gaining a strategic foothold in Asia by leading from the front. The broadcasting of Chinese economic influence and military strength is directing the course of geopolitics in Asia at a time when American foreign policy is undergoing shifts and revisions. It has left Beijing with the initiative to shape the nature of relations between states and the rules of engagement.

Significantly, if the ECS is to serve as a prototype for Beijing's policy choices, an aggressive and acquisitive strategy will follow in the SCS and Indian Ocean Region, to expand China's influence. However, the strategy has limited effectiveness and cannot sustain itself in the long run. By turning the Senkaku Islands into a hotspot for unrest, Beijing has made the actors in the region unsure of its decision-making. The limbo and uncertainty of consequences works in China's favour. China's rise has cautioned Japan into adopting a non-confrontational posture. Fears of antagonising China for the sake of regional stability have stalled the collision course which the Chinese foreign policy has embarked on.

Japan too has embarked on a course of strategic competition with China by investing in competition with Beijing and lobbying for support from other SCS disputants. Economically, Japan benefits from superior technology which will keep it relevant in the global economy, and the Chinese dependent on Tokyo. Japan is also considering the possibility of a blockade, and to insulate the economy from fluctuations in the availability of energy, Tokyo has begun to diversify its energy routes and sources. With respect to energy security in the ECS, China has the upper hand because it can continue exploiting hydrocarbon energy in the ECS. The ECS can yield benefits to Japan if Tokyo can secure a joint development agreement with China. However, repeated incursions and maritime aggression by China have caused Japan to expand the scope and capabilities of its armed forces. Additionally, Japan's domestic politics have developed to mobilise popular support against the Chinese, who are seen as aggressive. With Tokyo trying to match Beijing's moves and counter China's strategy, Japan is embarking on a course of remilitarising itself and standing up to China. The trajectory of Japan's policy and posture in the ECS is setting up the two nations for a clash in the ECS. Fortunately, Japan seems to be capable of resolving the dispute diplomatically.

China and Japan are locked in a stare-down contest to test the durability of alliances and the temperaments of other states in East Asia. A game of one-upmanship has the tendency to produce unforeseen consequences for regional stability. It cannot be sustained in the long term because it risks Beijing's economic credentials and relationships.

The following measures will help to restore stability in Sino-Japanese relations and halt confrontations in the ECS:
- A mechanism for dispute resolution in Sino-Japanese relations needs to be developed. This will go a long way in keeping the conflict from escalating.
- Negotiating Confidence Building Measures (CBMs) in times of conflict will ease mistrust, and instill confidence in the other's ability to do the right thing for the sake of regional stability.
- The CCP should not tolerate vandalism and rioting during anti-Japanese demonstrations. Protests should be allowed, but must not be tolerated if they turn violent toward Japanese nationals and Japanese economic interests.

- China can learn to emulate the Japan model of nationalism that is relatively well controlled by the state and does not hamper relations between states.
- A Code of Conduct should ease the frequency of infringements by the Chinese Navy and reduce the possibility of encounters between the PLAN and JMSDF.
- Tokyo must also look to defend itself without invoking the US alliance in times of tension, which has stirred Beijing's fears of containment by the USA. Similarly, China must also not involve Russia in the ECS dispute as a counterweight to the USA. China has reacted poorly to US involvement and Tokyo can improve its relations with China by building a bilateral relationship without elements that make Beijing anxious of Japan's intentions. Similarly, China must not invoke Russia and unsettle Japan.
- China can time its missile tests, joint sea exercises and other measures of power projection better. The CCP should hold back these activities on days on national importance, during state visits and other obviously significant days. Beijing must not pointedly display its indifference for Japanese concerns. Beijing's actions can ease Tokyo's fears by notifying it before conducting research near the Senkaku/Diaoyu Islands.
- China must also control fishing vessels entering the territorial waters of the Senkaku/Diaoyu Islands, and prevent nationalist groups from landing on the islands. Japan too, must look to do the same.
- Resolving the Senkaku/Diaoyu Islands dispute requires more than just restraint from both sides. Cooperation in the form of economic and commercial interests should be the foundation on which further confidence can be evolved.
- The large bank of cultural linkages should be mobilised

to foster trust and cooperation between the two states. Trade treaties and other formal partnerships between the two states will create a basis for understanding each other and display trustworthiness. Resource exploitation is one such base on which trust can be developed. Sharing data on hydrocarbons or having observers on oil rigs will go a long way to rest Tokyo's fears of China exploiting Japan's share of resources.
- Cooperating in the realm of energy security will ease the mistrust between both states and eliminate the fear of a blockade. With Japan and China investing in diversifying energy and self-developing sources, energy cooperation between both sides will benefit the ECS security structure and the respective economies.

Building confidence in the ECS must be the guiding principle of a process to restore regional stability. Shared responsibility would mean a coordinated attempt to provide logistical and security assistance to ships that are part of the trade and energy flows in the ECS. China and Japan would be responsible for the trade routes and energy supplies in the ECS through a joint maritime security force. It would arrest insecurity in the region by making China and Japan responsible for the security situation in the region. The two countries can agree on some form of shared responsibility, joint hydrocarbon exploitation and joint research facility for the Senkaku/Diaoyu Islands dispute. Hence, the islands would cease to have a military purpose. Revisiting the idea of joint exploration as was done in 2008 may calm the storm. It would alleviate the fears of Chinese aggression and reduce the insecurities of Japan's containment tactics.

China and Japan have to consider the possibility of coexistence in the maritime commons despite contradictory claims of ownership. Sharing responsibility in the ECS could be the path to conflict resolution if the region is not to become a cemetery for ships caught in the crossfire in the 21st century.

Notes

1. Central Intelligence Agency, "1971, East China Sea," Flickr, November 7, 2016, https://www.flickr.com/photos/ciagov/30583779680/in/photostream/.
2. Hong Kong Trade Development Council,Chinese Customs Statistics, 2016. Accessed on May 01, 2017, http://info.hktdc.com/hktdc_offices/mi/ccs/index_static_type/20MajorProductsnTop5Countriesexeng.htm
3. Sheila A. Smith, *Japanese Domestic Politics and a Rising China* (New York: Columbia University Press, 2015), p. 212.
4. Ibid., p. 113.
5. Ibid., p. 118.
6. Reinhard Drifte, *Japanese-Chinese Territorial Disputes in the East China Sea: Between Military Confrontation and Economic Cooperation* (Asia Research Center, London School of Economics and Political Science), LSE Research Online, 2008. Accessed on May 02, 2017. http://eprints.lse.ac.uk/20881/1/Japanese-Chinese_territorial_disputes_in_the_East_China_Sea_(LSERO).pdf. 21.
7. "China Q1 GDP Growth Accelerates at Faster than Expected 6.9% Annual Pace," CNBC, April 16, 2017, http://www.cnbc.com/2017/04/16/china-reports-q1-gdp.html.
8. Maggie Zhang, "China Rolls out Blueprint for Yangtze 'Global City-Cluster'," *South China Morning Post*, June 04, 2016, http://www.scmp.com/news/china/policies-politics/article/1964289/china-rolls-out-blueprint-yangtze-global-city-cluster.
9. "Key Industrial Parks in Yangtze River Delta", *Technical Paper*, November 21, 2011. Accessed on May 01, 2017, http://www.mortenson.com/~/media/files/pdfs/key-industrial-parks-yangtze-river-delta.ashx. 6.
10. Xiaoqing Zhu, Weijun Gao, Nan Zhou, Daniel M. Kammen, Yiqun Wu, Yao Zhang, and Wei Chen. "The Inhabited Environment, Infrastructure Development and Advanced Urbanization in China's Yangtze River Delta Region," *Environmental Research Letters* 11, no. 12 (2016): 124020. doi:10.1088/1748-9326/11/12/124020.
11. Nan Liu, "An Analysis of Competition Between Ports in the Shanghai International Shipping Hub," Report, Department of Management Science and Engineering , Zhejiang University, Zhejiang Provincial Social Sciences Foundation.

12. "China Sea Freight Shipping," *Cargo From China*, December 06, 2016. Accessed on May 01, 2017. https://cargofromchina.com/sea-freight/
13. Zhu, et. al., n. 10.
14. Liu, n. 11.
15. Ibid.
16. "Top 100 Ports," Publication 2016. Accessed on May 03, 2017, https://www.lloydslist.com/ll/incoming/article534477.ece.
17. Hong Kong Trade Development Council, 2016. Accessed on May 01, 2017. http://china-trade-research.hktdc.com/business-news/article/Fast-Facts/Shanghai-Market-Profile/ff/en/1/1X39VTST/1X06BVOR.htm.
18. Hong Kong Trade Development Council, 2016. Accessed on May 01, 2017. http://info.hktdc.com/hktdc_offices/mi/ccs/index_static_type/ExportsbyCountryofOriginFinalDestinationex.htm.
19. "World Shipping Council: Partners in Trade," Top 50 World Container Ports, World Shipping Council. Accessed on May 18, 2017. http://www.worldshipping.org/about-the-industry/global-trade/top-50-world-container-ports.
20. "Top 10 Countries/Regions by Trade Value and 5 Major Exports," Hong Kong Trade Development Council, 2017. Accessed on May 01, 2017. http://info.hktdc.com/hktdc_offices/mi/ccs/index_static_type/Top10countriesn5MajorProductsexeng.htm.
21. Ibid.
22. Malte Humpret, "The Future of Arctic Shipping: A New Silk Road for China," Centre for Circumpolar Security Studies, November 13, 2013. Accessed on May 05, 2017. https://issuu.com/thearcticinstitute/docs/the_future_of_arctic_shipping_-_a_n.
23. Ibid.
24. Rodger Baker, "Fish: The Overlooked Destabilizer in the South China Sea," *Stratfor Worldview*, February 12, 2016. Accessed on June 05, 2017. https://www.stratfor.com/article/fish-overlooked-destabilizer-south-china-sea
25. Feng Hao, "China," 中外对话 *China Dialogue*, August 24, 2016. Accessed on June 05, 2017. https://www.chinadialogue.net/article/show/single/en/9207-China-s-deep-sea-fishing-industry-relies-on-fuel-subsidies.
26. "China's Largest Fishing Port Celebrates its 600th Anniversary," *People's Daily Online*, November 20, 2009. Accessed on June 05, 2017. http://en.people.cn/90001/90782/6818751.html.
27. Micah Muscolino, "Overfishing Fuels China's Maritime Disputes," *The Third Pole*, January 09, 2017. Accessed on June 05, 2017. https://www.thethirdpole.net/2016/10/20/the-most-prized-fish-in-asia-drives-chinese-overfishing/.
28. Hong Zhao, *China and India: The Quest for Energy Resources in the 21st Century* (New York: Routledge, 2012), Accessed on May 05, 2017. https://books.google.co.in/books?id=LrntIU-iSrcC&pg=PA34&dq=East China

Sea energy supply routesChina&hl=en&sa=X&ved=0ahUKEwiWz7Cu_eX TAhWsAMAKHQDXDAMQ6AEIJzAB#v=onepage&q&f=false. 36.

29. Agnia Grigas, *The New Geopolitics of Gas* (London: Harvard University Press, 2017). Accessed on May 04, 2017. https://books.google.co.in/books?id=-DxYDgAAQBAJ&pg=PA382&dq=Exports from East China 2016&hl=en&sa=X&ved=0ahUKEwjCjPCmqMHTAhVLNo8KHTxTDew4 ChDoAQgnMAE#v=onepage&q=Exports%20from%20East%20China%20 2016&f=false. 237

30. Emily Meierding, "Don't Blame the Oil Rigs for the Unrest in the East China Sea," *TIME*, June 25, 2015. Accessed on May 06, 2017. http://time.com/3903411/oil-rig-resource-war-truth/.

31. US Department of Energy, Washington, "East China Sea," 2014, https://www.eia.gov/beta/international/regions-topics.cfm?RegionTopicID=ECS.

32. Ibid.

33. Ibid.

34. Ibid.

35. "In the East China Sea, China Crosses a Line," *Stratfor Worldview*, November 7, 2016. Accessed on May 19, 2017. https://www.stratfor.com/analysis/east-china-sea-china-crosses-line

36. Selig Harrison, "Seabed Petroleum in Northeast Asia: Conflict or Cooperation?" Wilson Centre for International Scholars, https://www.wilsoncenter.org/sites/default/files/Asia_petroleum.pdf.

37. n. 31.

38. Ibid.

39. Asia Maritime Transparency Institute, Report, October 14, 2016. Accessed on May 06, 2017. https://amti.csis.org/energy-competition-east-china-sea/.

40. "Sea Lines of Communication Security in the Asia-Pacific and the Arctic," China Institute, University of Alberta, 2014. Accessed on May 2017. https://www.ualberta.ca/china-institute/conferences/maritime-security/arctic-asia-pacific.

41. Malte Humpret, "Future of the Northern Sea Route," The Arctic Institute, October 2011. Accessed on May 2017. https://issuu.com/thearcticinstitute/docs/future_northern_sea_route.

42. Stockholm International Peace Research Institute, March 11, 2017. Accessed on May 2017. https://www.sipri.org/commentary/topical-backgrounder/2017/chinese-russian-energy-cooperation-arctic.

43. "China's Interest in Arctic Shipping," China Policy Institute, Analysis, March 12, 2015. Accessed on May 20, 2017. https://cpianalysis.org/2015/03/12/chinas-interest-for-the-arctic-and-arctic-shipping/.

44. Brad Lendon, and Katie Hunt, "China, Russia Begin Joint Exercises in South China Sea," CNN, September 13, 2016. Accessed on May 2017. http://edition.cnn.com/2016/09/12/asia/china-russia-south-china-sea-exercises/.

45. European Union, Institute for Security Studies, Michal Makocki Popescu and Nicu Popescu, "China and Russia: An Eastern Partnership in the Making?" December 2016. Accessed on May 2017. http://www.iss.europa.eu/uploads/media/CP_140_Russia_China.pdf.
46. US Department of Defence, "China Major Naval Units," Map, in University of Texas Libraries, US Department of Defence, 2012. Accessed on June 7, 2017. http://www.lib.utexas.edu/maps/middle_east_and_asia/china_major_naval_units-2012.png.
47. Hailong Ju, *China's Maritime Power and Strategy: History, National Security and Geopolitics* (Singapore: World Scientific Publishing Co., 2012). Accessed on May 2017. https://books.google.co.in/books?id=Hxm3CgAAQBAJ&pg=PR35&lpg=PR35&dq=offshore waters defense strategy geopolitical terms&source=bl&ots=Sv8QGLeURm&sig=govYEphqMwecVWhdSYkrfy8BK4w&hl=en&sa=X&ved=0ahUKEwiXv9P5g_7TAhVERo8KHaCzA08Q6AEILzAB#v=onepage&q=offshore%20waters%20defense%20strategy%20geopolitical%20terms&f=true.
48. Geoffrey Till and Patrick Bratton, *Sea Power and the Asia-Pacific: The Triumph of Neptune?* (London: Routledge, 2013). Accessed 2017. https://books.google.co.in/books?id=D2OpAgAAQBAJ&pg=PT99&dq=PLAN anti access East China Sea&hl=en&sa=X&ved=0ahUKEwjWzvDi0fPTAhVLPY8KHWLoBzE4ChDoAQg_MAU#v=onepage&q=PLAN%20anti%20access%20East%20China%20Sea&f=false.
49. "Chinese Jets Intercept US Aircraft Over East China Sea, US says," BBC News, May 19, 2017. Accessed on June 29, 2017. http://www.bbc.com/news/world-asia-china-39971267.
50. Vinayak Bhat, "China Builds New Coast Guard Ships," ORF, N.p., April 2017. Web. May 22, 2017.
51. Anthony H. Cordesman, Steven Colley, and Michael Wang, *Chinese Strategy and Military Modernization in 2015: A Comparative Analysis* (Washington, DC: CSIS, Centre for Strategic & International Studies, 2016), Pdf.
52. Enrico Fels, and Truong-Minh Vu, *Power Politics in Asia's Contested Waters: Territorial Disputes in the South China Sea* (Cham: Springer, 2016), Pdf.
53. Ibid.
54. Lars Assmann, *Theater Missile Defense (TMD) in East Asia: Implications for Beijing and Tokyo* (Münster: Lit Verlag, 2007, Google Books, 2007), Web. May 2017. <https://books.google.co.in/books?id=rRfpAgAAQBAJ&pg=PA290&dq=lasers, particle beam weapons and high powered microwaves CHina&hl=en&sa=X&ved=0ahUKEwjg1ciF1ILUAhWBPI8KHQzdA-4Q6AEIITAA#v=onepage&q=lasers%2C%20particle%20beam%20weapons%20and%20high%20powered%20microwaves%20CHina&f=false>.
55. "Military and Security Developments Involving the People's Republic of China," Publication, Office of Secretary of Defence, 2010. Web. May 2017.

<https://books.google.co.in/books?id=o8p8Zk2pNrMC&pg=PA36&dq=beidou 2 2020&hl=en&sa=X&ved=0ahUKEwj786HS1ILUAhXItY8KHYpYBT8Q6AEIITAA#v=onepage&q=beidou%202%202020&f=false>.
56. Ibid.
57. Cordesman, et. al., n. 51.
58. Ibid.
59. n. 55.
60. "Internet Users by Country (2016)," Internet Live Stats. Accessed on May 22, 2017. http://www.internetlivestats.com/internet-users-by-country/.
61. Deepak Sharma, "Integrated Network Electronic Warfare: China's New Concept of Information Warfare", *Journal of Defence Studies*, vol 4, no 2, April 2010, pp.36-49.
62. Jason Fritz, "The Semantics of Cyber Warfare," Report East Asia Security Centre, Bond University, November 29, 2013. Accessed on May 2017. http://epublications.bond.edu.au/cgi/viewcontent.cgi?article=1041&context=eassc_publications.
63. Ibid.
64. Phil Muncasater, "Chinese Hacktivists Launch Cyber Attack on Japan." *The Register*, September 21, 2012. Accessed on May 2017. https://www.theregister.co.uk/2012/09/21/japan_china_attack_sites_senkaku/.
65. Jeevan Vasagar, and Geoff Dyer, "Chinese Hackers Targeted US Aircraft Carrier," *Financial Times*, 2017. https://www.ft.com/content/b03bc7f0-9745-11e6-a1dc-bdf38d484582.
66. Franz -Stefan Gady, "Japan Hit by Cyberattacks at an Unprecedented Level," *The Diplomat*, February 20, 2015. Accessed on May 2017. http://thediplomat.com/2015/02/japan-hit-by-cyberattacks-at-an-unprecedented-level/.
67. "Japan Parliament hit by China-based Cyberattack," *The Telegraph*, October 25, 2011. Accessed on May 22, 2017. http://www.telegraph.co.uk/news/worldnews/asia/japan/8848100/Japan-parliament-hit-by-China-based-cyber-attack.html.
68. Cordesman, et. al., n. 51.
69. Justin McCurry, "Japan Anxious Over Defence Data as China Denies Hacking Weapons Maker," *The Guardian*, September 20, 2011. Accessed on May 2017. https://www.theguardian.com/world/2011/sep/20/china-denies-hacking-attack-japan.
70. James Andrew Lewis, "US-Japan Cooperation in Cybersecurity," Strategic Technologies Programme, Centre for Strategic and International Studies, November 2015. Accessed on May 2017. https://csis-prod.s3.amazonaws.com/s3fs-public/legacy_files/files/publication/151105_Lewis_USJapanCyber_Web.pdf.
71. Sheila Smith, "Intimate Rivals: Japanese Domestic Politics and a Rising China". Place of publication not identified: Columbia University Press, 2016.

72. Ibid.
73. Peter Dutton, *Scouting, Signaling, and Gatekeeping: Chinese Naval Operations in Japanese Waters and the International Law Implications* (Newport. RI: China Maritime Studies Institute, U.S. Naval War College, 2009). http://www.andrewerickson.com/2009/02/scouting-signaling-and-gatekeeping-chinese-naval-operations-in-japanese-waters-and-the-international-law-implications/.
74. Ibid.
75. "China is Planning a Massive Sea Lab 10,000 Feet Underwater," Bloomberg, June 8, 2016, https://www.bloomberg.com/news/articles/2016-06-07/china-pushes-plan-for-oceanic-space-station-in-south-china-sea.
76. "Chinese Offshore Oil Rig Deployed to East China Sea," RWR Advisory Group, September 3, 2014. Accessed on June 05, 2017. http://www.rwradvisory.com/chinese-offshore-oil-rig-deployed-to-east-china-sea/.
77. Smith, n. 71.
78. Ibid.
79. John Pike, "Military," Ieodo / Suyan Rock / Socotra Rock. Accessed on June 05, 2017. http://www.globalsecurity.org/military/world/war/socotra-rock.htm.
80. Yang, Huiping Xu, Changwei Xu, and Rufu Qin, "A Study of the Remote Control for the East China Sea Seafloor Observation System," *Journal of Atmospheric and Oceanic Technology* 29, no. 8 (2012): 1149-158. doi:10.1175/jtech-d-11-00115.1.
81. Eugene C. LaFond, "East China Sea," *Encyclopædia Britannica*, May 01, 2017. Accessed on June 06, 2017. https://www.britannica.com/place/East-China-Sea.
82. "China Is Planning a Massive Sea Lab Almost Two Miles Underwater," NextBigFuture.com, April 06, 2017. Accessed on June 06, 2017. https://www.nextbigfuture.com/2016/09/china-is-planning-massive-sea-lab.html.
83. Ibid.
84. Antoine Roth, "Conflict Dynamics in Sino-Japanese Relations: The Case of the Senkaku/Diaoyu Islands Dispute," PhD diss., George Washington University, 2013. ProQuest. 3. http://pqdtopen.proquest.com/doc/1417776652.html?FMT=AI.
85. Alan Taylor, "Anti-Japan Protests in China," *The Atlantic,* September 17, 2012. https://www.theatlantic.com/photo/2012/09/anti-japan-protests-in-china/100370/.
86. "China's Anti-Japan Protests: Keeping the Automaker Damages at Home," *East Asia Forum,* September 20, 2012. Accessed on June 06, 2017. http://www.eastasiaforum.org/2012/09/21/chinas-anti-japan-protests-keeping-the-automaker-damages-at-home/.
87. Keith Bradsher, "Amid Tension, China Blocks Vital Exports to Japan," *The New York Times,* September 22, 2010. Accessed on June 06, 2017. http://

www.nytimes.com/2010/09/23/business/global/23rare.html?hp.
88. "Understanding Chinese Nationalism: Historical Memory in Chinese Politics and Foreign Relations," YouTube video, 10:20, posted by The Woodrow Wilson Centre, April 23, 2013, https://www.youtube.com/watch?v=xN8BPecpNZg.
89. "Interpreting Protest in Modern China," Advertisement, *Dissent Magazine*, Winter 2011. https://www.dissentmagazine.org/article/interpreting-protest-in-modern-china.
90. "China's Expanding Core Interests," Uyghur American Association. Accessed on June 06, 2017. https://uyghuramerican.org/article/chinas-expanding-core-interests.html.
91. Swetha Ramachandran, "Capturing the Growth of Digital Nationalism in China," East Asia Research Programme. Accessed June 06, 2017. http://earp.in/en/capturing-the-growth-of-digital-nationalism-in-china-2/.
92. Erik Beukel, "Popular Nationalism in China and the Sino-Japanese Relationship," Report, 2011. https://www.files.ethz.ch/isn/126613/RP-2011-01-China-Japan_web.pdf.
93. Kazuyoshi Nishikura, "Reexamination of the Process of the Enactment of China's Territorial Sea Law—Internal Conflict over the Specification of the Senkaku Islands," Report, Ryukyu University, March 2017. https://www2.jiia.or.jp/en/pdf/digital_library/world/170331_nishikura.pdf.
94. Ibid.
95. Ibid.
96. Ibid.
97. Japan, Ministry of Foreign Affairs, Foreign Policy, http://www.mofa.go.jp/region/asia-paci/senkaku/qa_1010.html.
98. Japan, Ministry of Foreign Affairs, Position Paper 2, Surrounding the Senkaku Islands Situation, December 8, 2012. http://www.mofa.go.jp/region/asia-paci/senkaku/position_paper2_en.html.
99. "East China Sea Tensions: Approaching a Slow Boil," Asia Maritime Transparency Initiative, April 14, 2016. Accessed on June 13, 2017. https://amti.csis.org/east-china-sea-tensions/.
100. Shiro Armstrong, "Economics Still Trumps Politics Between Japan and China," Report Crawford School of Public Policy, Australia National University, Vol. 634, International Affairs. https://www2.jiia.or.jp/en/pdf/publication/2014-09_003-kokusaimondai.pdf.
101. Ibid.
102. Haier, News and Press, "Haier Sets up Asia HQ in Japan," News release. Haier.com. http://www.haier.com/my/newspress/announcement/201203/t20120330_120927.shtml.
103. Sonali Paul, and Narayanan Somasundaram, "Mitsubishi seen Tapping Chinese for Australian Iron Ore," Reuters, February 19, 2012. Accessed on June 26, 2017. http://www.reuters.com/article/us-mitsubishi-oakajee-

idUSTRE81J06U20120220.
104. Jennifer Muncher, "Toyota Build New Headquarters in Beijing." *The Automotive News Updates*, Accessed on June 26, 2017. http://www.automotiveheadlines.com/toyota-build-new-headquarters-in-beijing-1341.html.
105. Armstrong, n. 100.
106. Michael Fitzpatrick, "Did China Steal Japan's High-Speed Train?" Fortune.com. April 15, 2013. Accessed June 26, 2017. http://fortune.com/2013/04/15/did-china-steal-japans-high-speed-train/.
107. Leslie Lopez, "China, Japan Jostle for Lead Role in Singapore-KL Rail Project," *The Straits Times*, April 11, 2016. Accessed on June 26, 2017. http://www.straitstimes.com/asia/china-japan-jostle-for-lead-role-in-singapore-kl-rail-project.
108. Ralph Jennings, "Japan is Becoming Player in South China Sea Sovereignty Dispute," VOA, March 23, 2017. Accessed on June 26, 2017. https://www.voanews.com/a/japan-player-south-china-sea-sovereignty-dispute/3773376.html.
109. Headhoncho, "Cofinancing with Japan." Asian Development Bank. February 02, 2017. Accessed on June 13, 2017. https://www.adb.org/site/cofinancing/japan.
110. "Japan: Rising Direct Investment in Southeast Asia," DBS Bank, DBS Group Research, March 18, 2016.http://www.dbs.com/id/personal-id/aics/pdfcontroller.page?pdfpath=/content/article/pdf/aio/160318_insights_japan_looks_to_southeast_asia_for_growth.pdf"
111. Yun Sun, "Rising Sino-Japanese Competition in Africa," Brookings Institution, August 31, 2016. Accessed on June 26, 2017. https://www.brookings.edu/blog/africa-in-focus/2016/08/31/rising-sino-japanese-competition-in-africa/.
112. Ibid.
113. "Commentary: Abe Tries Again to Ram Self-Serving Priorities into Agenda of International Meeting," Xinhua | English.news.cn. August 29, 2016. Accessed on June 29, 2017. http://news.xinhuanet.com/english/2016-08/29/c_135642772.htm.
114. "Investment in ASEAN," CEICdata, December 14, 2015. Accessed on June 26, 2017. https://www.ceicdata.com/en/node/494.
115. "Japan is Trying to Court Influence in Southeast Asia Through ODA," *Global Times*. Accessed on June 26, 2017. http://www.globaltimes.cn/content/930920.shtml.
116. Linda McCann, "Japan's Energy Security Challenges: The World is Watching," Report, Centre for Defence and Strategic Studies, Australian Defence College, October 2012. http://www.defence.gov.au/ADC/Publications/Commanders/2012/08_SAP%20Linda%20McCann%20-%20Japan.pdf.

117. Ibid.
118. "Japan's Energy Supply Security," Report, International Energy Association, http://www.iea.org/media/freepublications/security/EnergySupplySecurity2014_Japan.pdf.
119. "Security Through Renewables," Report, Institute for Energy Economics and Financial Analysis, http://ieefa.org/wp-content/uploads/2017/03/Japan_-Greater-Energy-Security-Through-Renewables-_March-2017.pdf.
120. Japan, Ministry of Economy Trade and Industry, Meti.go.jp. http://www.meti.go.jp/english/press/2016/0624_03.html.
121. Reuters, "Japan Government Draft: Nuclear to be 20-22 Percent of Power Mix by 2030: Media," *Business Insider*, April 23, 2015. Accessed June 26, 2017. http://www.businessinsider.com/r-japan-government-draft-nuclear-to-be-20-22-percent-of-power-mix-by-2030---media-2015-4?IR=T.
122. "GSSG Solar Announces Financial Close and Ground-breaking of Suwa, Nagano Japan, 47 MW Solar Plant," Solar Asset Investment, Advising and Acquisitions. Accessed on June 26, 2017. http://gssgsolar.com/suwa-nagano-japan-47-mw-solar-plant/.
123. Total, "ISE Group, Total and SunPower Start Up the Nanao Solar Power Plant in Japan." ISE Group. Accessed on June 26, 2017. http://www.total.com/en/media/news/press-releases/ise-group-total-and-sunpower-start-nanao-solar-power-plant-japan.
124. Reinhard Drifte, "Territorial Conflicts in the East China Sea – From Missed Opportunities to Negotiation Stalemate," *Asia Pacific Journal*, 3rd ser., 7, No. 22, May 25, 2009. http://apjjf.org/-Reinhard-Drifte/3156/article.html.
125. US Department of Energy, Washington, "East China Sea," 2014. https://www.eia.gov/beta/international/regions-topics.cfm?RegionTopicID=ECS
126. "Flows of Inward Direct Investment to ASEAN," Advertisement, ASEAN Stats, October 5, 2016. https://data.aseanstats.org/fdi_by_sector.php.
127. Yonaguni, Reuters In, "Japan Extends Military Reach in Disputed East China Sea," *The Guardian*, March 28, 2016. Accessed June 13, 2017. https://www.theguardian.com/world/2016/mar/28/japan-extends-military-reach-yonaguni-disputed-east-china-sea.
128. Emanuele Scimia, "Japan's East China Sea Military Build-up Continues," *The National Interest*, May 6, 2016, http://nationalinterest.org/feature/japans-east-china-sea-military-buildup-continues-16087.
129. Lyle Morris, "The New Normal in the East China Sea," Rand Corporation (web log), February 27, 2017, https://www.rand.org/blog/2017/02/the-new-normal-in-the-east-china-sea.html.
130. Ibid.
131. Ankit Panda, "Japan's Izumo Helicopter Carrier to Escort US Navy Supply Ship," *The Diplomat*, May 01, 2017. Accessed on June 13, 2017. http://

thediplomat.com/2017/05/japans-izumo-helicopter-carrier-to-escort-us-navy-supply-ship/.
132. Jennings, n.108.
133. US Department of Defence, "First and Second Island Chain," Map. University of Texas Libraries. 2012. Accessed on June 7, 2017. http://www.lib.utexas.edu/maps/middle_east_and_asia/china_first_and_second_island_chains-2012.png.
134. David McNeill, "Japan's Southwest Territories Being Militarised Amid Rising Fears of Rising Superpower China," *The Irish Times*, July 29, 2013. Accessed on June 26, 2017. https://www.irishtimes.com/news/world/asia-pacific/japan-s-southwest-territories-being-militarised-amid-rising-fears-of-rising-superpower-china-1.1477669.
135. Bjørn Elias Mikalsen Grønning, "Japan's Military Response to a Shifting Strategic Environment," Report, Centre for Asia Security Studies, Norwegian Institute for Security Studies. https://www.atlcom.nl/ap_archive/pdf/AP%202014%20nr.%205/Gronning.pdf.
136. "The Road to Revising the Pacifist Constitution," *The Japan Times*, Accessed on June 26, 2017. http://www.japantimes.co.jp/opinion/2017/05/11/commentary/japan-commentary/road-revising-pacifist-constitution/#.WU-zjWiGNPY.
137. Sugio Takahashi, "Japan: Revising Security Legislation and the Japan-US Defense Cooperation Guidelines," 54-55, *East Asian Strategic Review*. http://www.nids.mod.go.jp/english/publication/east-asian/pdf/2015/east-asian_e2015_01.pdf.
138. Grønning, n. 135.
139. Ibid.
140. Chrystopher S. Kim, "Nationalism: The Media, State, and Public in the Senkaku/Diaoyu Dispute," PhD diss., Naval Postgraduate School, 2015. http://calhoun.nps.edu/bitstream/handle/10945/45206/15Mar_Kim_Chrystopher.pdf?sequence=1.
141. "Hostile Neighbors: China vs. Japan," Advertisement, Pew Research Center. 2016. http://www.pewglobal.org/2016/09/13/hostile-neighbors-china-vs-japan/.
142. Kim, n. 140.
143. Tomohiro Osaki, and Kikuchi Daisuke, "Abe Declares 2020 as Goal for New Constitution," *The Japan Times*, May 3, 2017. Accessed on June 26, 2017. http://www.japantimes.co.jp/news/2017/05/03/national/politics-diplomacy/abe-declares-2020-goal-new-constitution/.
144. David McNeil, "Nippon Kaigi and the Radical Conservative Project to Take Back Japan," *The Asia Pacific Journal*, December 14, 2015. http://apjjf.org/-David-McNeill/4409.
145. Yang Lijun, and Lim Chee Kia, "Youth Nationalism in Japan and Sino-Japanese Relations," Report, East Asian Institute, National University of

Singapore. http://www.eai.nus.edu.sg/publications/files/Vol1No2_YangLijunLimCheeKia.pdf.
146. Robson Seth, "Conservative Japanese Lobby Group Seeks to Revise Constitution," *Stars and Stripes,* July 18, 2016, Accessed on June 26, 2017. https://www.stripes.com/news/conservative-japanese-lobby-group-seeks-to-revise-constitution-1.419654#.WVFRr2iGNPY.
147. Ming Wan, Google books, 2006. https://books.google.co.in/books?id=VF9UEemebUoC&pg=PA41&lpg=PA41&dq=lighthouse built on islands Japan&source=bl&ots=4Bk75x_e2X&sig=yaz1fXgLDR96F-883yiq4iyF55o&hl=en&sa=X&ved=0ahUKEwjZ-MLxquLUAhXKipQKHdUdDW04ChDoAQguMAQ#v=onepage&q=lighthouse%20built%20on%20islands%20Japan&f=false.

www.ingramcontent.com/pod-product-compliance
Lightning Source LLC
Chambersburg PA
CBHW021358300426
44114CB00012B/1277